The Unwoven Tapestry Of Love

By Sherri Christy

Dedication

~I want to dedicate this book to my sons whom I love with all my heart! You guys have been my driving force to stay on a path of determination. I wouldn't be the best version of myself without the both of you being in my life! To my Mom who has been my constant supporter. I love you! Lastly, but not least to God who has kept me afloat in this world and who has caused me to see myself like He does, a Victor. I give you all the glory~

The Unwoven Tapestry of Love

Acknowledgements

I would like to acknowledge Mr. Fletcher for all the long hours and the hard work that you put into helping make this book come to life. Your kindness and patience were a godsend. My endless thanks!

To the Godhead that has stuck with me during the hardest times of my life and who has taught me that being strong was always possible. My endless love is yours~

And lastly but not least, to all the Pastors, mentors and friends that have stood with me through all my sufferings and trials, Thank You!

Table of Contents

Preface

You know my name but not my story! Which makes me truly glad that you have glanced through my book. I hope you will take it home with you and not put it down until you've read every page. As you begin the journey with me I'll start off by briefly taking you through my childhood first, so you can see where my roots began. Then you'll discover the type of family background that I came from and lastly, you'll follow me along the path of my adult life. Each chapter will escalate with hidden secrets that my own family and friends have never known about me, until now.

As you turn each page there will be times that you will experience various emotions such as laughter, love, anger, heartache, and pain with me. You may even relate to some, or all these emotions that I've experienced because maybe the same thing has happened to you. If so, then that's why you picked this book up. Just know that we can navigate through any problems that are taking place right now in your life because there is always a solution and I want to share that with you! It's all about us going through this life together, so we can heal and move forward and lead people towards the Light.

So, if by spilling my guts out along the pages of this book in the most transparent way that I can touches one's life through my personal tragedies, experiences, and victories, then I have done what my life's purpose was to do and that is to help others heal. Let this book richly envelop you, lessen your pain, heal your hurts, fill you with encouragement and strengthen you for the journey ahead. My hope is that it gives you the confidence to face another today, so that tomorrow will be even better and your future so much brighter.

That's the reason I wrote this book…. For you!

I call this poem Starfish:

There was a young man walking down a deserted beach just before dawn. In the distance he saw a frail, old man. As he approached the old man, he saw him picking up stranded starfish and throwing them back into the sea. The young man gazed in wonder as the old man again and again threw the small starfish from the sand to the water. He asked, "Old man, why do you spend so much energy doing what seems to be a waste of time?" The old man explained that the stranded starfish would die if left in the morning sun. "But there must be thousands of beaches and millions of starfish!" exclaimed the young man. "How can you make any difference?" The old man looked at the small starfish in his hand. As he threw it back into the safety of the sea, he said, "it makes a difference to this one!"

-Author unknown-

~ We are all a starfish to someone. Be encouraged~

-Sherri

Introduction

Throughout these pages I want to offer you the chance to see through someone else's eyes, to walk in someone else's shoes for a moment so that you know you're not alone regardless of what you may be going through right now.

As an author, I am extremely honest and raw in how I write because I want the reader to understand the whole truth not the half-truths or leave you hanging without answers as to how I made it through so many crises. I believe that my life has been on an uncommon journey since I was born and that it has been filled with so many obstacles and road blocks that have tried to hinder me from moving forward.

Do you know that If I had given in to any one of those detours, I wouldn't be here right now? So, to prove that my circumstances were not what my life was truly based upon, I wrote a book on how I overcame every one of these hindrances so that you too can be an overcomer. This life was not given to us, so we could live defeated!

I believe that every one of you who picked this book up did so because you can relate to at least one of these categories that I have written about. Situations relating to feeling rejection as a child, being hurt by a relationship(s), abuse of drugs or alcohol, sexual addictions, divorce, abortion, loss of a child, touched inappropriately or suffer from an illness. Please know that this is the right book your holding in your hands.

I recommend this book not because I'm the author but because I have stories that you need to hear so that you too can find you're release in this lifetime. I don't want you to waste one more minute. I want to share with you the struggles that I have dealt with in my life as well as the victories. So that you know there is good news and that I have moved forward regardless of anything that has ever tried to make me quit, and you can too, I promise!

Every trial that we face is another stepping stone to our learning and growth process. This process elevates us to the next level in life. Soon you will have the opportunity to help someone else by what you have been acquainted with in life and have overcome yourself. Nothing is ever counted as a loss, if what you have been through has taught you a valuable lesson and has matured you.

Growth is inevitable. Whether it is motivated by good or bad circumstances happening in your life. The world continues to move on its axle whether we want to keep up with it or not. Everything happens for a reason, everything has a season, a purpose, a time to live and a time to die. A time to begin and a time to end. Life is a cycle, and yes at times vicious but the choice to shine again is always yours and no one can take that away from you.

In this book we will journey through my childhood, and my teenage years, then go into my adulthood. I will show you the unwoven tapestry of love that was there amidst the pain. You will witness firsthand the heartache and devastation that should have destroyed me, yet you will also see the way these things have shaped my journey and has turned me into someone else. Someone that I've always wanted to be. Come with me, won't you?

~Those who get through the struggle, go on to become "Victors", by prospering from the process~   -Sherri

Chapter 1- Being a child
(the innocent years)

I was born on the anniversary of J.F.K.'s death and that should have spoken volumes already as to how my life was going to play out. God knows I have been at risk since the first day I entered this world. When I was delivered from my mother's womb I was only eight months old. During my mother's generation when a baby was to be delivered earlier than its due date there was an incredible risk to the baby's health. While my mother was in labor, the doctor discussed with her the risks that were associated with me being born at only eight months old. This was because I was in between cycles and transitioning into the ninth month. He also told her that there may be complications during my delivery. Back then the hospitals didn't have all the fancy gadgets or the technology that we have today. But I made it!

I was not one of those children who had the privilege of having both of their paternal parents around. My parents only got married because my mother was pregnant. Their marriage didn't last very long. When I was around age two my mother caught my father in bed with their best friend. The one who always liked to buy me beautiful frilly dresses. That alone should have been an indicator to alert my mother that something just didn't seem right. You see my mother and father's best friend was a man! After my mother witnessed this incident she immediately kicked my father out of our home.

I never saw him again. It turns out that my father had his own demons to deal with while being psychologically challenged. And because he was being exposed as a homosexual he probably had about all that he could take. I never knew how he really felt about me because I didn't get to see my father after the day he disappeared. I think in his mind he warred with the fact that he wasn't sure if he was truly a homosexual or not. And because he wasn't sure about his sexuality he had decided to try and date a woman to find out. That woman was my mother. This led to a pregnancy and then marriage. It's probably not any sequence of events that he intended to ever have happen, but it did. I also believe that God doesn't make mistakes and that I was meant to be here.

The biggest blessing to come from my father was that I got to know my grandmother and her husband. They were a big part of my life as a child and with plenty of visitations came lots of fun stuff like crafts. In my heart, I never believed for a moment that my grandmother was trying to take my father's place. Her love did make up for the difference though. I don't think it was a coincidence that she became a part of my life at such a crucial time but that it was necessary since my biological father was not around. As time went on I lost contact with her because we moved a few times and so our paths never crossed again.

I hadn't thought about my father since the time he left. I was growing up and reaching my pre-teen years. My life was getting exciting and I was too filled with love from my mother, step-father, and family to miss someone I didn't even know. There was no need to feel sad or empty about the situation. In all honesty, I had forgotten about him. It wasn't until many years later at the age of twelve that my mother presented me with an opportunity to see my biological father. Immediately I declined the invitation. I can still recall our conversation going back and forth between my mother and I as I sat in the backseat of her car watching her intently focus on the road. She never once glanced back at me in her rear-view mirror to look at my face. All she said was that he wanted to see me, and the choice was completely up to me. I never changed my answer to yes and I never saw my father again. I found out shortly afterwards that he had died. He was only in his early forties.

Could this have been his last dying wish to see his daughter? Possibly. As a budding teenager, who couldn't care less about someone who never took an interest in me, I just didn't want to see him. At least that's what I thought back then. As teenagers, we think we know everything, right? I didn't know that he was sick when I was posed with the question to see him or not. I didn't realize then that he may have wanted to right some of the wrongs that he had made. I didn't understand what forgiveness was. I was a rebellious teenager who had thoughts embedded in my brain of how I never existed in his world before, so why now? I figured at the time I didn't need anything from him and I certainly wasn't interested in what he had to say. Yet as an adult, if I could go back and change my mind knowing what I now know, I probably would have met with him and at least have listened to what he had to say. I'm grateful that my mother never lied to me about his life. I truly believe that it helped me not to blame myself for all those missed years with him.

It wasn't too long after that my mother had met my step-father, so I never went without a father's love or a father figure in my life. Their relationship lasted for many years and was nothing like what had happened with my real father. I got to see a whole other side of love. My stepfather raised me until I was eighteen and had graduated from High School. There was only one time that a separation occurred between the two of them. They did manage to reconcile before I left home to venture out on my own. My stepfather was so handsome, he reminded me of a cross between Elvis Presley and Dean Martin and he had the drinking habits of both men. He had shiny black hair with a flip on the front of his forehead like he was from the 50's. His complexion was olive toned. He taught me to love music. He drove a deep green colored Cadillac and ran a roofing business out of our garage. This is where I use to pretend that I was his secretary. I can't remember a time when he ever raised his voice at me or gave me a spanking. He loved me like his very own and never treated me as a step-child. His heart was gigantic and warm, and he was always patient with me.

I'll give you an example. On one of my childhood incidents, me and my best friends brother was down in the basement of our home. My friends brother who I was playing with at the time asked me to pull my pants down, so I did. Then he pulled his down. We weren't doing anything but looking at each other. We were too young to know how to do anything sexual. I guess he was curious to see if all girls looked like his sister did. My mother happened to be upstairs and came down to the basement to finish hanging up the laundry on the clothes line. When she saw our half naked little bodies she ran through the wet clothes that were blocking her view and screamed, "What are you two doing?" As if she had just seen a horror show! As I realized the frantic look on her face I knew we were in big trouble even though I wasn't sure why. Immediately my mother pointed the finger and sent me upstairs. Then the uncontrollable crying started coming from my sobbing lips as I ran like lightening to my room.

After my emotional rollercoaster episode ended I could hear the voices of two women coming from our kitchen. They were both discussing our punishment. When my mother came in to tell me how long I was punished for, it seemed like a life sentence! My stepfather was so gracious about it all. He knew that I was innocent and having pity on me, he came into my room and sat me on his lap and said don't worry I will make sure you get out to get some fresh air. My punishment lasted for a month. My stepfather kept true to his word. He would take me on trips to do errands with him. He would let me take control of the steering wheel so that I could drive on the back roads of our town to get my mind off being punished. I was so grateful for his acts of love. In my heart, he was the only father that I ever had. He always showed me mercy and would come to my rescue.

At about age six my parents enrolled me into a Catholic school and I was introduced to God. Both my mother and stepfather were not religious at all but were the exact opposite. I have no idea how I wound up attending Catholic school. It was the first time I was ever exposed to nuns and God. In grade school, I was on the student body and was exhibiting signs of leadership in my early childhood. It was also my first experience with going to church. Both the teachers and nuns were amazing people. I remember two of them that stand out in my mind the most. One gave me a book of poetry with her signature in it. I wonder if she knew I was going to write in my future? She was a good influence on my life. There was another nun who had reddish hair like I did, and she would always take the time to acknowledge me. She used to call me carrot top. I never took offense because she had the same color hair that I did. I think she was teaching me at a very young age to be prepared for the teasing that I would have to endure due to having red hair. This was another small affection of love that I never forgot about.

I had some knowledge of God as a child. Although I didn't understand the whole concept of who this God was. I always said my prayers. I don't even know how I learned to pray. I had a beautiful necklace with charms consisting of a bible and the Pope that I admired. I would talk to God a lot especially at night when I was not able to sleep, was afraid or when I got sick. Nobody in our family was religious. No one took me to church accept when

I attended chapel at school. My only other experience with going to church was when my cousin would take me with her.

My grandmother baptized each one of her six children a different religion but we all called ourselves Catholic because that seemed to cover all the religions. I used to pray the famous children's prayer. "Now I lay me down to sleep I pray the Lord my soul to keep, if I should die before I wake, I pray the Lord my soul to take." I did that every night. The prayer was posted above my bed. I still have the scroll packed away somewhere. For some reason doing this made me feel closer to God.

My first true experience with God revealing himself to me as a child was quite interesting. It was when I was walking home from elementary school. I was no longer attending catholic school. I was around age nine. Suddenly I had this urge to look up into the sky. As I looked up I not only saw blue sky and clouds, but I saw two angels standing right in front of me. There they stood two angels one on each side of what looked like white gates that were opened wide and then the whole picture disappeared as quickly as I saw it appear. When I arrived home, I was made aware that my best friend, Sylvester who was our Siamese cat had died. I will never forget what I saw that day in the sky. It truly was a sign that God was speaking to me. I was being prepared for an experience with death and God was reassuring me that Sylvester was in Heaven. The gates that I saw signified an entrance into another world. I knew it was other worldly because Angels existed there.

The passing of my cat was much different than my other episode. My first experience with death as a child was with a pet fish. I was devastated because I had never been exposed to death before. So, when I was told that we should flush the fishy down the toilet I was in tears. I thought we can't do that and let it go out to sea! My alternative was to get an old shoebox and put the fish in it. Then go out to the backyard, dig a hole, say a few nice words and bury it. I chose the alternative. This too was heart breaking but at least I knew where my fishy went. Sylvester the cat was more like losing a part of my family. This experience took much longer to get over than the first one but now I was exposed to how death worked, and I was aware of its finality. I knew there was a place to go to after people and pets died.

Up until then there's not a whole bunch of significant memories that I can recall. I don't remember much of my childhood except for a few things. Like the time I got a hold of some matches and nearly burned the house down. Boy, was I in trouble. My mother was dumbfounded at how a five-year-old knew how to light matches. Then at the age of seven my stepfather taught me how to ride my first bike. It didn't turn out like I'd hope. I ran right into a huge tree located on the corner of our block and hurt my pubic bone. I hadn't experienced that kind of pain before. It made me want to never ride a bike again! It took me quite some time before I would even think about getting on a bike.

One great memory that I'll never forget about is when my friends and I used to run around in my back yard at dusk and catch lightening bugs and snapping turtles. My backyard was so huge it seemed like a wildlife preservation filled with bugs and reptiles. We always had family and friends over for BBQ's. No party went without liquor or a keg of beer at every function. If there was a holiday or an occasion to party, we would celebrate. I have three aunts and two uncles. My mother was the oldest of six children. Everyone always attended our yard parties. I enjoyed being surrounded by so much love at this age. In my innocence, I was never aware of the problems people were having because I was too young to understand. As children, sometimes we are protected from that stuff and I am glad that I was.

While growing up I spent a lot of time at my grandparents' house from my mother's side. My mother worked two jobs. So, they became my babysitters. My cousin also went to our grandparents when her mother worked. I kind of grew up with my cousin. We were just like sister's beings we were together a lot. We were around the same age and grade. I didn't have any siblings. My grandmother had six children. There were more than enough kids in the house to keep us busy. During the winter times when it snowed my grandmother would tell my cousin and I to go outside and gather up some snow, so she could make us a bowl of sugary vanilla snow ice-cream.

Of course, no yellow snow was allowed. My grandmother was amazing. She constantly cooked, raised six children, took care of her grandchildren, worked, and rarely ever drank. She also never drove a car. If anyone could earn the name super-woman, it would be her. She was in the foster care system as a teen. Then met my grandfather and they got married. As an adult, she managed to keep her family together. It wasn't an easy road. My grandfather was quite a character and an alcoholic for most of his life. He used to play store and church with us when he was drunk and in a good mood. He was excellent at figuring out and fixing electronic things. I do want to mention that before my grandfather passed away he did get sober. I miss you pop-pop!

It felt to me as if I practically grew up over their house. We used to watch my aunt iron her long hair on the ironing board and we would wrestle with our uncle. We had so much fun with them. My cousin would always tell on me when I did something I wasn't supposed to do. One day she dared me to go and pee behind our neighbor's car. It was parked in the drive way, so no one could see me except for her. She told me to go first. So, I squatted behind the car and started to urinate and immediately she ran into my grandmother's house and told them. I was punished after that incident. My cousin says she doesn't remember this, but I do. I must say I always felt like the outcast between the two of us. I mean I guess someone had to, right? I was sort of the black sheep. I was always getting punished or caught doing things I shouldn't have been doing. I guess it was like what real sisters would have gone through.

I was active in school and got involved with gymnastics, girl scouts and bowling. I tried to stay out of trouble for the most part. I didn't realize at this point that I was any different from any of the other kids. I liked to pretend that I was a teacher. In my bedroom, I had a blackboard that I would write my assignments on. My stuffed animals were my students. I used to pretend that my bedroom was my classroom. My mother made me a nun outfit for Halloween one year and I loved it! I would dress up as a nun almost every day. This is what I did most of the time when I was home. I usually played alone if I wasn't with my cousin.

I wasn't spoiled even though I was an only child. I did get the things that I wanted though. I've learned so much from my mother who taught me a valuable principle. Which was when she had the money I would get what I wanted and not beforehand. I learned to wait and be content with what I had. It taught me how to be grateful and not too be hastily with money. Yes, I wore designer jeans and Nike sneakers and birthdays and Christmas were a time for overloading on gifts, but I always shared what I had with others.

I was beginning to transition into my adolescent years. Going from age twelve and onto thirteen. I started to recognize that I had a gift of knowing what someone was thinking, or I could read what number was on a playing card that someone was holding in their hand. I didn't pay too much attention to that at the time. Until I got older.

My last memories of being a child were not eating what was made for dinner, so I had to sit there until I finished every bite. Has this happened to you? I had to sit in front of a bowl of turkey noodle soup for what seemed like an eternity until I finished every bit because my mother wasn't going to cook anything else. I stopped eating turkey soup for a long time because of that. Of course, now I love turkey soup!

A couple of things that used to freak me out when I was a kid was when my friend would put potato chips in her PB&J. I don't know why but for some reason I wouldn't eat PB &J's for a long time. Another creepy thing that happened was when I stuck my hand in a brown paper bag and something was moving around inside it. Before I could get my hand out it crawled up my arm. It was a water bug! It took me years to finally open a bag, I screamed for days! Can you remember stuff like that? Did it traumatize you? Lol.

Overall, I had a normal childhood. My family most definitely had its share of problems. What family doesn't? I didn't focus on any of that as a child because I wasn't required to fix adults problems. Unbeknownst to me then was that as I became an adolescence some of their problems did become my problems. Most children have not been exposed to have to understand hardships nor should they be. If they have been then they aren't sure why it's happening to them or their family. It's important for them to know that whatever is going on inside of a household that it is not their fault and they are never to be blamed.

Lesson Learned: We don't get to pick our parents. Period. So, we should never harbor the guilt of their short comings or for the choices they have made while we were in their care. We don't have to make the same mistakes as they did either. It's never too late to redirect your life and make the impossible things possible by making the necessary changes to heal your heart. Do away with repetitious patterns and start writing the new chapter of your life and who you are becoming now. Honesty is the best policy and it will set you free, you can heal from the truth faster than to be weaved in a web of lies and never knowing the truth which can leave open wounds. Never sell yourself short. You deserve to know the truth. Remember choices are just what the word says they are and they are subject to change. We learn from the choices we have made and continue to make, let your past choices teach you. Make new choices from the wisdom you have gained. Remember although someone is not a biological parent it does not exclude them from becoming one to someone else. Being a biological parent is just chemistry between two people. It takes a dedicated human being to love another person unto themselves unconditionally. It also takes an act of being responsible. I don't want to say you earn the name parent but that you become deserving of the role when you truly take on the task of raising children. Lastly, never think your alone! There is a God and He will show Himself to you to help you through your difficult moments. Just ask Him too. Take a moment right now to look back on only the good memories of some one that showed you little acts of love in your childhood. Like I did with the nuns and my step-father. Remember those that stand out in your mind and who have made a difference. Pray that you could be one of those people who will stand out in the life of someone else. Forgive so that you will have peace in your heart. Childhood is an inevitable part of your life and it cannot be overlooked. You must go through this stage first to reach adulthood. What has shaped you as a child whether it be good or bad will carry on into your adult life if you allow it to. That's where many of our lives get messed up. Release those hurts and pains that may be holding you back to becoming the whole person you were meant to be. Forgive those who did you wrong for they may not even know what they did or don't even remember. Start your journey to healing now and begin the newest cycle of your life so that you may have joy. Make a list so that you can acknowledge the people who weren't the best advocates in your life and one by one release them through forgiveness. Then make a list of people to praise for being there and who made a difference in your life. If you have never acknowledged them then do so now. Share that love! Maybe through a thank you note or by giving them a call to express your thoughts towards them. A merry heart does good like a medicine. You'll probably make their day. There is such empowerment in the releasing of people. Then relax, breathe, and laugh at all the bizarre things that now seem magical.

Ephesians 1:5 – God decided in advance to adopt us into His own family by bringing us to Himself through Jesus Christ. This is what He wanted to do, and it gave Him great pleasure.

Chapter 2- Not a Little Girl Anymore

(best friends, boys & rejection)

I was twelve when I got my first menstrual period. I was so excited I had to tell my mother. I think every girl wants to tell someone when that moment comes. We had moved into our new home. I was attending another school and getting ready to connect with new friends. I was now in middle school. As I was getting older I started to notice things for what they were. There were no more excuses like when I was little. I began to realize the different behaviors that certain family members displayed, and the effects alcohol had on them. My grandfather was an alcoholic and so was my stepfather. I started to see the influence it had on people that I loved and how they would change into a happy or sad mood when consuming alcoholic beverages.

In this season of my life I was into the arts, poetry, dancing and acting. I had a Jewish teacher who recognized my talents and he used to tell me that my parents should put me in a school for the Arts. I often wonder how very different my life could have been if I was enrolled. I wasn't concerned with boys yet. I never had a boyfriend. Well, except in second grade. This boy used to bring me gifts from his home. We eventually found out that he was stealing the gifts from his mother and sisters. That put a damper on his charming ways and I ended that quickly. I did things like the other kids. I started going skating. I went to the mall and had sleepovers. I wasn't hanging out in my room playing school as much anymore. That seemed childish to me now. I was still innocent, a virgin and not tainted by other people's behaviors. Yet!

When we moved into our new home I met this girl in my neighborhood who quickly became my best friend. She was quite beautiful. She looked like the kind of girl that I always wanted to be. She didn't come from a rich family. She had a lot of brothers and sisters, so she would sleep over my house when she could. No one bothered us because if they did her older brothers would beat the daylights out of them. We had a lot of things in common such as her father and my stepfather were both alcoholics and we understood the lifestyle. By being together it helped us escape all that nonsense that we had to deal with.

We would wear matching outfits and shoes. We'd go to the arcade, malls and skating together. We had innocent fun. We were starting to understand what becoming a woman was by doing our hair and using makeup. She was aware of how beautiful she was. Yet she never bullied me when it came to my looks. Not like the boys started doing because I wore glasses and had red hair. Believe me the red headed step child syndrome was at work in my life. I had both. Red hair and a step-father. I can affirm that being a red head with glasses was not easy and the rumors are all true. Today red hair is stylish but back in the day it was taboo.

It didn't take long for us to notice boys. It wasn't soon after that she gained a boyfriend. I started to separate from her and began to hang out with people who were considered "the bad crowd." I started to dye my hair bleach blonde to change the red color and hide the fact that I was a redhead because I was tired of getting teased. I also switched to contacts because I was upset at being called four eyes all the time and because the boys kept stealing my glasses. I was called names; my tube tops would get pulled down and the boys used to steal my bike. They would ghost ride it into the walls or hills. To them it was hilarious but to me it hurt deep down inside. But I acted tough. I didn't want them to think I cared what they did to me.

I was the type of person who had friends from all different kinds of back rounds. I didn't care what they looked like, the color of their skin, their religion or whether they were rich or poor it didn't matter to me. I am still the same way today. I would be friends with whoever I wanted to be. I used to have people say to me why do you hang out with so and so or why do you talk to them? My reason was because I understood what being rejected felt like. I knew what it was like to have someone not like you because of the way you looked. I had no intentions of hurting other people the way I had been hurt.

I learned the hard way how to respect people. In high school, I hung out with druggies, jocks, preps, and dropouts. I had a friend from each group. I guess I learned something from the whole red headed syndrome. From then on, I never wanted to stereotype or make fun of anyone. In fact, I was friends with people who had no friends just because of this very reason. I could sympathize with people who were bullied. When I was being rejected and boys were teasing me I used to go and hang out with the poorer girls in my community. It was probably because everything that I went through they could relate to. I recall having a friend that lived down the street from my grandmother's house and she was poor. Her house was filled with cock-roaches and they lived like hoarders. My grandmother would say "stay out of her house" because it was dirty. I believe God was putting things into my heart as a young girl to show me how to love people that were different, poor, and needy. To this day, I still do. I was not poor; we were middle class and doing well. But I felt that I always connected better with these girls. People mattered to me more than myself and material things.

Now don't get me wrong I wanted to be like the pretty girls and the snobs. I wanted what they had, and I wanted to look like they did. I didn't want to stand out as a red head with glasses. That is why I covered up my identity with cosmetics. To be honest, trying to be something that I wasn't, made me miserable. I was so miserable that I even contemplated suicide. One night I stood in my bathroom in front of the mirror and said I can't take this anymore while holding a bottle of pills. Thank God, I was too chicken to do it! But there are others that have not been so fortunate and who have taken their own lives because of an identity crisis.

I don't believe it's uncommon today that girls are still suffering from fitting in with the status quo. I have seen some beautiful women call themselves ugly. It all begins from within first. When we get that right we will then see ourselves beautiful on the outside. We all want to be that beautiful princess and remain forever young, but the reality is that we weren't all born with a naturally beautiful face or long flowing hair like the models portray. So, we get to the point where we want to start disfiguring our faces so that we can look a certain way to attract a certain person and we want that quick fix. But that isn't who we were created to be. Now I'm not saying you shouldn't take care of yourself or try minor procedures to help certain areas of your face or body but to keep scarring who you are makes the inside of you feel worse.

You will think each time you fix something that it is not good enough and you will never reach your expectation of how you think you should look. You'll never feel loved nor will you be able to find true love. You will continue to live dysfunctional and you will attract those very same people to yourself repeatedly. It all begins within you! The only people that change are the people that make it happen. The ones who welcome it. You won't ever reach your full potential do to the same obstacles that continue to keep popping up in your life. Let's stop pointing fingers and let's start talking to ourselves first. Let's start with positive affirmations and the fact that we are creative, smart, able, etc.... Let's keep declaring this daily so that our minds start to believe it! Let's weave love into our souls for ourselves first.

We really can't fully comprehend how to love someone else with a genuine love until we first learn what loving ourselves looks like. Even when we must deny ourselves certain things because they are not good for us. We must learn to recognize that and master how to say no to the bad things and yes to the good things. This is how we start to become confident in our decision making. This is where we become free and comfortable in being who we were created to be by giving ourselves the permission to change for the better.

In my high school years, I liked everyone but myself. I had a lot of friends, yet I still wasn't happy with the way I felt on the inside. I started smoking cigarettes at the age of nine. I was interested in boys at twelve and I started smoking marijuana and drinking alcohol. I felt like I wasn't accepted because of the way I looked. So, I made the decision to be like other people and by doing that I would get accepted by doing the things they were doing. I had a need to fit in with people. We all have that need, the question is at what cost? I always felt like I was different. I was unique. I had my own style of dress. I didn't act like the other girls because inside I was genuinely wanting to be me. I did not want to pretend to be someone else. This is how clicks form. You must be just like the other girls to fit in otherwise you can't be their friend. Oftentimes, I felt very different from other girls because of my looks and it seemed like the whole world was staring at me all the time, where ever I went. I didn't look like others because most people didn't have red hair and glasses back then. I begged my mom to wear makeup and get contacts. I didn't want to be unique! So, when my mom finally agreed, I started to develop my own style and look by changing my appearance.

I love hair, makeup, clothes, and shoes. As a young girl, I started mastering the art of makeup. I loved to use different colors and try new things especially on other people. My cousin would let me practice on her face often. I wanted to be a beautician until I found out that you had to study the whole cranium and the inside of it. Instead, I put my focus more on boys, that was easier to do. I was more interested in being accepted.

Now that I'm an adult I know how blessed I truly am to be who God created me to be. That I am unique because I got to know what God thought of me. At the time, I was a teenager I never knew I needed healing from this dilemma. I didn't realize that all along God was working out my talents in my teenage years because I didn't know about Him nor did I understand why He made me.

I wished back then that someone would have told me sooner why I was created the way I was because there was a specific journey planned for my life and that no matter what, it would all work out if I believed that it could. I needed that support when I was struggling and was being made fun of. I needed to be told that I was different for a specific purpose. That I was creative. I wish someone had told me that there wasn't anything wrong with me because I didn't look like everyone else. So, if your reading this and you are struggling let me tell you now: You are special! Loved! Unique! Set apart for a specific journey. No one else can do what only you can do. Your meant for greatness and to touch other's lives. To pay something forward! To contribute your talents to society. Don't ever let the opinions of others tell you otherwise. You know the enemy will use people to get you off track. To keep you as a damaged good and label you as undeliverable. Let me be the first to tell you none of it's true! The enemy lies! He kills and will destroy your purpose if you let him.

I'll be honest. I still don't approve of everything about myself. I am aging, sagging, and getting wrinkled but I don't lose focus on what is more important. Me being beautiful on the outside or how I can make a difference in the world by me being whole on the inside. Can I help others by staying broken? Or can I lead others to victory by overcoming. Today I know that I am an artistic person, not by any means an average person. One who is talented and who has something to tell others. I know now that being different is quite beautiful. I take my creative abilities now and put them to use. I don't buy into the lies anymore because they have wasted to much of my valuable time. God showed me who I really am and that changed everything!

I have learned to accept people for who they are because frankly we can't all be supermodels! I just continue to thank God for makeup and lotions that I can use to enhance my features. Then I stay focused on what I do like about myself. Both inside and outside. Then I'm content to be me. Just because I'm not a supermodel doesn't mean I'm not beautiful both on the inside and the outside. The same goes for you too! The beauty of someone else is found in the eye of the beholder but your true worth is always found from the treasures within.

Lesson Learned: You don't need a mirror to tell you who you really are. Your outer shell is not the final say. Could you imagine how much more self-confident we all would be if we had no idea what we looked like on the outside? I think we would appreciate each other's differences more. If you don't like who you are on the inside, then that is where you start first. Rejection often causes us to shy away from who we are due to how others have treated us. Whether it was because people bullied us, or our family members didn't treat us the way we deserved. Maybe it's because they disrespected us by telling us that our life was worthless. For whatever reasons, these people that have crossed our path are not the final say in who we are just like the mirror isn't. God created you and gave you a purpose from the very beginning of your life. It had nothing to do with the way you looked because we are all made in His image. You must seek out what that is to truly become confident again if you have lost this confidence. Even if you are model material on the outside it doesn't mean you're happy from within. The truth is that there is going to be someone out there who does think your beautiful just the way you are. I learned how to accept a person for who they were and not to judge them by their outward appearances because outward appearances can lie. Some of the most outwardly beautiful people are very ugly on the inside and unhappy. Everyone needs someone to love or to be loved by. We were created out of love and for love. God is love! It is a vital part to life. People have broken hearts and broken lives because no one has ever let them know they are loved. So never give up on yourself. Start loving yourself. The reality is that you can try as hard as you want to change your outer appearance to look like the latest fashion guru's picks but afterwards if it doesn't suit you or feel right you won't be happy. Life is more than using cosmetics, alcohol, or drugs to help hide your real identity crisis problem. It is about contentment in knowing that you were uniquely made and that there is no one else like you. Unless you are an identical twin or a triplet. Even then you still have your own personality. You must be you because you were made as an original! The one and only. No one else has your thumb print. There is no carbon copy of you! Never think that you are disposable because you don't match up to someone else 's wrong expectations or twisted thinking of who they think you should be. People that hurt others have most likely been hurt by someone as well. Which makes them less likely the standard that you need to be measured by. Look at the good qualities that you possess and work on bringing them to the forefront of who you are. You were created in the image of God and He is beautiful! If you look around the world there are creatures both great and small all uniquely made and beautifully hand-crafted in their own rights. They were created unique and with purpose. Just think if we all looked alike we wouldn't be able to tell each other apart. We couldn't bring our uniqueness to the world with all our ideas, teaching's, or inventions. We wouldn't have the light bulb, or telephone to speak into. Modern cell phones would not exist. Oh, gosh! Take a moment to reflect on the magnificent qualities that you do possess. Then be thankful for them. Gratitude changes everything! Practice on yourself. Make a list of the good qualities that you possess. Then put them into every day practice. Choose one to do for a week or a month at a time. Do it long enough until you recognize the greatest parts of you that do exist! If you say, "I don't know what they are?" Then start observing yourself to find that out or create something new from within. You can do it. I'm rooting for you!

Ephesians 3:18 – And may you have the power to understand, as all God's people should, how wide, how long, how high, and how deep His love is.

Chapter 3- My Introduction to Dating
(drugs, alcohol & bad influences)

I previously mentioned that my family members drank except my grandmother. My grandfather and stepfather were both alcoholics. The difference between my stepfather and grandfather was that my grandfather stayed at home to drink while my stepfather went to bars. Most of my stepfather's friends were alcoholics so if they weren't at the bar they were over our house. My stepfather would host poker parties in our basement. I would wake up some days and find at least one of my stepfather's friends on our couch. I grew up going to a bar practically every other night with my stepfather and mother. When we did visit the bar, I would be in my own little world. I'd pretend I was an adult. I would order my dinner which usually consisted of cheese steaks and Shirley temples which I loved. I would do my homework and then take breaks. I'd get a bunch of quarters to use in the pinball and video game machines to pass the time. Then upon departure we somehow got home safely every time. It had to be divine providence.

My mother drank but she liked mainly to be with her sisters and friends. Everyone would take turns hosting a party at their place. I grew up going to these parties almost every weekend. The party would start out with some appetizers. Then people would start drinking. The music would slowly escalate from being soft to a loud club like sound. Donna Summer was the ambience throughout the house. Then when they were drunk everyone would start dancing to songs like the Rubber Band Man and Copa Cabana. We knew when this started to happen it was our chance to jump all over the furniture and the beds. It literally became a chaotically fun situation for us kids. We loved it!

Other times when my mother and step father would go out alone they would leave me with a babysitter. My one babysitter was the daughter of my stepfather's friend. What my parents didn't know was as soon as they left the house it would quickly fill up with people, alcohol, and drugs. My babysitter would blast the stereo by playing Led Zeppelin while people broke out their addictions of choice. By her hosting these parties at my house is how I became accustomed to hanging around with older people. I started to develop an interest for what the older generation was doing. I had no idea that it was wrong except that I wasn't supposed to be doing it yet.

I was introduced to drugs, alcohol, and men at an early age. I had my first crush on this guy we will call Sam. He was so cool and smooth. He was more of the hippie type. Although no one ever took the time to talk with me he did. I remember how he would pull out this unpainted wooden box that he'd carry around with him everywhere he went. It was his trademark. Everyone knew what was in the box. He carried all his paraphernalia, a bong, marijuana, lighter and cigarettes in this box. He was one of the go to guys to get high with. I didn't realize that his lifestyle was abnormal and that most families did not live this way because I was constantly around it. This became a huge part of my environment and it seemed normal to be around these types of people. Although they never pushed anything on me.

During this time, I was about nine or ten and I started to hang out with an older girl who moved into the corner house. As soon as she moved into the neighborhood we quickly became friends. She was a black girl, but it didn't matter to me. Even though the people in my neighborhood didn't want other races to live in our town, I didn't care. I will call her Mary. Mary became a bad influence on me fast, but I really liked her. She taught me how to smoke cigarettes. Mary was about sixteen. We used to hide out in my fort that my step-dad built for me. He owned a roofing business and with the left-over supplies from his job he had constructed a little shed for us. It was here that we would smoke, listen to music, and hide all our stuff that we didn't want our parents to find. I would ask my mom for money, so we could go buy cigarettes. Back in the day there were no age limits on buying cigarettes. The store owners figured we were coming to the store for our parents. That gave us the freedom to experiment with all brands of cigarettes. Occasionally I would go over to her house to eat dinner with her family. Eventually she moved because the neighborhood people ran them out of town. I believe we had some of the Ku-Klux Clan living amongst us.

One night I saw orange flames burning through an erected wooden cross on Mary's front lawn through my bedroom window. I was horrified! This also scared the hell out of them and they moved out of the neighborhood immediately. I lost my good friend. Even though Mary was not in my life the cigarettes still were! Now I was addicted.

It wasn't long before another family moved into the neighborhood. They had two older daughters that I became friends with fast. They had long flowing hair and both were very popular. Their home became my second home. They treated me like their little sister. They were almost twice my age. They would share their beauty regimens with me and taught me how to take care of my hair. The younger of the two sisters happened to be dating the boy I had a crush on. One day I was sneaking down the basement of their home. The younger sister was with the boy that I had a crush on and they were kissing. She caught me spying on them and said, "Sherri you are cramping my style!" I was so hurt that she was kissing the man that I had a crush on. Not to mention the tone of voice that she talked to me in, it caused me to slowly depart my friendship with her. From these relationships, I learned at a young age how to mature quickly. I learned I may not be able to trust other women and that racism was real. I also picked up some bad habits such as smoking cigarettes.

I could go wherever I wanted to if I checked in at dinner time and did the dishes. I had to be in when it started to get dark outside. At age nine I was already smoking cigarettes and by age eleven I realized that my parents had a liquor cabinet in our home. The liquor cabinet was always locked but I knew where they hid the key. I found it by snooping. They hid the key in the upper chamber of the cabinet where it didn't lock. It housed the drinking glasses where the key could be found. I had many avenues to get liquor. I was getting it from home and I was also getting it from the older people who I was starting to hang out with. When we would have family functions it was so easy to take alcohol from the refrigerator. As the night progressed and everyone was getting drunk it was then that I would sneak to the refrigerator and take some beer out for me and my friends. No one suspected a thing. This was another way to consume alcohol. I had access to it almost all the time.

I started to hang out with boys more than girls. I would frequently visit one boys house. I eventually started dating him. He taught me how to French kiss, introduced me to MTV and taught me how to smoke marijuana. I was about eleven years old. I never had a real boyfriend before. I was still a virgin. The only boy that I ever kissed was a redhead when I was seven and in grade school in my shed. He came to my fort one day and he kissed me. Although I didn't like him, I did want to know what a kiss felt like. Eventually, me and the boy who taught me how to French kiss broke up.

I started seeing this other guy. He was popular among the girls. I don't know why but I started to fall in love with this guy quickly who we will call Bret. He was older than me and he had a girlfriend, but he used to cheat on her all the time. The girl he was dating was also popular in school. He knew he had a good girl and didn't want to ruin the relationship, so he made sure that she didn't catch him cheating. Eventually he and I started an ongoing relationship. I am not using the word date because it was never that. We used to party all the time together. I was always hanging out with the older crowd. When we got drunk that is when we'd wind up together but not in front of people. We would go off somewhere else alone and of course people knew what was going on, but they never said anything. I was a secret from his girlfriend. No one ever told her. I think she had an idea though.

I don't know why but for a couple of years I allowed this to go on. What did I know about love? I guess I thought maybe after a while he would eventually call me his girlfriend. I started to notice that he would have other girlfriends out in public but not me. When his girlfriends weren't around him he would be with me in secret. I finally smartened up and started seeing other people. He pretended that it didn't bother him because he never asked me to stop seeing them. It was like a big game. What a crazy relationship I was having. I was only twelve years old and my heart was being crushed. I thought I loved this guy. I guess because he even dared to take the risk to be with me in secret in my mind I thought I must have mattered to him. Like as if he was taking a big chance on being with me.

This went on until I was about fourteen. I never had sex with him as a teenager and I am glad that I did not. It was the only dignity that I had left. No matter how much I thought I loved him I never gave up my virginity because it wasn't worth it. Somehow, I knew in the back of my mind that it would be wrong to do. I think that if I did give that part of my body away it would have made matters worse for me. I must say that he never forced me to give myself away either.

I think back on all those times that I'd sneak out just to be with him. Now I realize how much of a mistake I had made.

Our time together mostly dealt with smoking pot and drinking, then we would make out for a while and he would go back to his nice warm cozy bed. I would lie to my parents and tell them that I was sleeping over a friend's house, but I was really over his house. I eventually stopped doing that because I got caught by my grandmother sneaking out one night. I don't advise anyone to ever be so naive. No one ever taught me the difference between love and lust. My mom wasn't the birds and bees type of person. I guess it made her feel funny discussing those things.

This very same guy used to call me names and belittle me in front of our friends. Then he would apologize later when we were alone. One night he was so drunk he put a cigarette out on my face in front of everyone at the party. He said he was trying to hit my glasses and missed. I was so humiliated that I left. If someone is just using you for whatever reasons, you need to recognize it quickly. If anyone disregards your feelings and doesn't care for your welfare you had better run! Even though I was on drugs and drinking alcohol I knew something wasn't right about our relationship. The worst part was when one day I was over his house and he had his friend over. This friend was also someone I knew. They both had decided to take me over to another room where it was dark. They made it seem like they were going to show me something or play a joke. As if I should trust them. They had locked the door so that no one could enter. They proceeded to tie my hands and my ankles with rope. Then they placed me on the floor. They used both their hands and took turns covering my mouth, so no one would hear me scream as they both took a turn putting their hands in my pants and fondling my private parts. It was mostly his friend doing the touching. I don't know if they were drunk or on drugs, but it was still no excuse for what they were doing.

I was so scared and crying. Finally, I heard the guys mother calling him for dinner. I guess they got worried. They didn't want his mother to come and see what they were doing with me, so they quickly untied the ropes. He left the room and the other guy followed him. I ran so fast out of his house and I kept running until I got all the way home. I was so frightened. I know God was watching over me that day. I had never seen them act that way before towards me. It was scary.

I have never told anyone about the incident until writing this book. I think it's important for people to know about these things. That's why I'm sharing my stories with you. Don't ever wait to tell someone if this happens to you! No one in my household had a clue about what happened to me. My parents had no idea. My grandparents and my uncle who lived with us didn't know. My grandfather and stepfather were both alcoholics as I mentioned before. My mom was a drinker. I wouldn't call her an alcoholic. My grandmother would stay in her room and so did my uncle, so no one knew what the other person was doing. No one was communicating except at dinner-time. I don't think anyone sensed what was starting to happen to me and if they did they never said a word.

I was now a teenager who started using marijuana and alcohol a lot. It became a daily habit of mine. It was what I looked forward too every day. I was still a virgin. That was the only thing left undefiled that I was in control of. Although that didn't stand in the way of me being with men in other ways. I just did it on my own terms. I could get away with coming into the house stoned or drunk because I would go straight to my room. Everyone else was already in their rooms or drunk so they never noticed how high or drunk I was. I was matured for my age because I hung out with mainly older people. I knew a lot more than the average Joe and how to hide stuff from people.

I believe this was where the root of rejection started to creep into my soul. It happened because I was being mistreated by someone who I thought cared about me, but he really didn't.

He was dysfunctional himself. I also had secrets that I thought I couldn't share with anyone else. I was being rejected and rejecting myself. I wasn't strong enough to handle the situation. I didn't know how. This guy hid me while he was seeing other women, let his friends touch me inappropriately, would humiliate me in front of other people and all because he was popular. He wanted both worlds them, and me. He never let me go but he had to mistreat me and act like a big shot in front of his friends because I was younger. I guess I thought I was special because he kept coming back for more. It was a terrible lie that I told myself. I was being teased and mistreated by boys for so long that I gained a complex about myself and what better way to cover it up than with alcohol and drugs.

We moved once again to a new town. My mother and step father had split up and I was now in the presence of another stepfather whom I hated! I would hardly attend school. I was starting to fail miserably. I did not want to get up in the mornings and if I did I would pretend that I was going to school and then cut classes. I would go and get drunk with the new friends that I had made. I even started to introduce pills into my daily routine.

To get alcohol now we would hide out around the side of a liquor store and randomly ask people to go and get liquor for us, some did, and some didn't. When we did score our alcohol, we would then retreat to the woods and hang out there until we got drunk or the police officers chased us out. I started dating men of all ages it was mostly older men. I dated a man that was thirty when I was fifteen. I didn't care I just wanted to drink and do drugs with them and drive in their cars. I never gave up my virginity though. It wasn't until I was fifteen that I finally gave in.

I was nearing the end of being fifteen. It was a few months before my sixteenth birthday and I caved. I still remember that night. I was dating a guy for quite a while and I started to fall for him. One night he invited me over to his parent's apartment, so we could have sex, without my knowledge. I just thought he was being romantic with all the lit candles and the soft music playing in the back-round by Marvin Gaye. After a little food and some beer, I found myself in his bedroom engaged in sexual activity that didn't go over very well. This was the first time I was ever sexually active with a man and I wasn't aware of the pain associated with having sex for the first time. I quickly retreated and ran to the bathroom and I vowed never to have sex again. It was traumatic for me to experience this for the first time in my life. I was bleeding and in pain. I didn't know what was happening to me. I couldn't tell my mom. There was no one to talk to or share my experience with and no one told me what to expect. I never had the birds and the bees talk. That was an experience I have never forgotten! Let's just say the guy wasn't very happy with me so I left.

Shortly after this episode the guy broke up with me. I don't know if it was because I wouldn't have sex with him again or what, but he started dating someone else. For the second time in my life my heart was broken. This break up was much worse because I had given an intimate part of my body away. It caused there to be a soul connection that made me love him more. It was just the opposite for him because he got what he wanted. My mother was a witness to my heartache, but I couldn't tell her why this one hurt so bad because she liked the guy and allowed me to date him.

I was the one hurt by losing my virginity not the man who took it from me. Apparently to him it was important to be with a virgin. He got pure satisfaction while I ended up alone in the end and crying my eyes out. It made my heart calloused towards love.

After we broke up I started to have a crush on a musician. I thought he was the hottest thing around and so did the other girls. I thought I was in love. So once again I gave in. My mother and new stepfather had gone away for the weekend. They said no one is allowed in the house. Of course, I disobeyed and had a huge party. I had everyone over. There was alcohol, drugs, and men. This guy that I liked happened to show up at my party and we wound up sleeping together. He had a girlfriend. I knew her. I didn't care. I had sex with him anyway. This time I liked it. We were both drunk and chalked it up to a one-night stand. I never hooked up with him again. I remember his girlfriend and our other friend yelling outside of my bedroom window telling him to leave because they knew he was inside with another girl but that didn't stop him from getting what he wanted. I was finally ok with that type of relationship. To me no one got hurt. This was my new way of thinking after all the abuse that I've experienced. I thought that if men can act that way so can I.

I started dating this older guy. He introduced me to LSD, a hallucinogenic drug. I was only fifteen. I wound up loving it too much and took it often. He wasn't the best-looking guy, but he was well liked, and he had a great body. He was very intelligent. He would lavish me with gifts and take me home to his parents for the holidays. His mother loved me. Then he started to get very possessive. He was starting to tell me what kind of clothing I should wear and how to wear my makeup. He always wanted to know where I was. I wasn't having it. I was too rebellious to listen to someone trying to tell me how to act. I was not going to let someone start running my life now.

My friends and I both liked the fact that he drove. He would give us rides everywhere. We did drugs in his car and had sex there too. My girlfriends loved the fact that I was dating a guy with a car and that they got to smoke weed all the time and hang out with the older crowd which they loved to do. I mainly tried to hang in there with him but due to him being so possessive I had to break up with him. He wouldn't accept the fact that I broke up with him and he wouldn't leave me alone. So, when I ignored him he threatened to commit suicide if I didn't take him back. The problem was that he was talking to a girl who had been rejected for years by men and she didn't care if he was being rejected now. I showed no response and eventually after months went by he left me alone.

When I did get into a relationship I sometimes found out that they were cheating on me. Like the one guy who was dating a girl who had the same name as I did but she spelled her name with a Y. One day we both showed up at his house for a party and he knew he was in trouble. I guess he forgot which Sherri, Sherry, he invited? So far, I was not experiencing respect, love, or commitment from any man. Of course, we were young. No one wanted to be committed. Therefore, in the future chapters you'll read and understand why I took the guy of my choice whenever I wanted to have sex and a good time and then didn't bother with them again after one night. I didn't want a commitment with anyone and I surely didn't want to keep getting hurt repeatedly. It took a while before I got into another relationship.

When I did get into new relationships it was always with men who had girlfriends or wives already, so I never maintained any solid relationships. I did this on purpose, so they wouldn't get attached to me. I did get to sleep with some of the popular men around the neighborhood, but nothing ever turned into a love story. Once your heart continues to get broken repeatedly you start believing that love stories aren't real.

Meanwhile, I had to experience the stepfather from hell. I watched my mother also go through an abusive relationship. He was so jealous of my mom that she wasn't allowed to go anywhere without him except for work. I used to come home drunk and stoned and I would beat the hell out of him. I hated him and the way that he treated my mother. She wouldn't defend herself, so I did it for her. I couldn't stand to watch my mother be with someone who was so possessive of her. It wasn't normal. Especially after I just experienced a similar situation in my past relationship because he was insecure. I wasn't about to let this guy treat my mother the same way.

The only good thing that came out of the relationship with my mom's new husband was that he had a child who I cared for. I don't think I was a good influence as an older sister though. I used to have my friends come in our bedroom that we shared, and we would smoke marijuana and drink beers in front of this child before going out. I didn't think of how I was affecting this person's life or what a bad example I was being. It was a cycle that I grew up around and was taught to me. This child use to witness the many fights that my mother and her husband would have but I wouldn't allow him to treat my mother with disrespect when I was there, and he knew it. It was all so dysfunctional. Eventually everything changed, and they wound up splitting up. My mom finally came to her senses after the family bothered her about it enough times and she left him.

My mother was the opposite of me she liked to be in committed relationships. She was a very classy woman who had a good head on her shoulders, who had a good job and was successful. She was with my first stepfather for over sixteen years and then had a relapse with the other guy from hell. She wasn't the type to be in a lot of relationships and I admired her for that. She was always self-sufficient, a good mother and a good wife. I guess that is why I was shocked to see her being de-humanized by this other guy, thank God it ended about three years later. We were all happy for her.

It didn't matter where we moved I always found the crowd who I could do drugs and drink alcohol with. It doesn't matter where you go these types of people are everywhere. I was being introduced to more drugs and incorporating them into my daily routine. I was now involved with crack and cocaine. I finally met someone who I genuinely liked, and we wound up staying together for many years until I cheated on him. By now I was so involved in every drug except heroine. I thank God that I never touched it. I thank God that I never wound up as a pregnant teenager. This guy's family member used to distribute drugs, so we had drugs at our disposal 24 hrs. and 7 days a week. We were doing it all the time and staying up all night long. I was used to being around drug dealers at this point because he would introduce me to them. I had a cocaine dealer tell me that if I wanted to be his girl he would take care of me forever. I was never afraid to be around the drug dealers just the police officers.

The first time my mother found out I had anything to do with drugs was when I got in trouble with the police. I was in a car with nothing but male friends. Suddenly the police officers were behind us and flashing their lights and immediately everyone handed me all their stuff and said you're a girl they won't check you. Like a fool I listened, and they found paraphernalia on me and locked me up. I had to call my mom and she had to come get me from the police station. I was punished for a long time. I told her that I was just holding the guys stuff and that I wasn't doing anything, but I don't think she bought it. I slept for a whole day after that night and my friend had to pour water on me to get me up. I was a complete mess.

After my mother ended her other relationship with the guy from hell we moved in with my mom's sister and her two kids. I was happy because I got to be with my cousin again but this time our relationship seemed different. My cousin and I was two completely different people now, then when we were little. She had become a prep and I was a druggie. She hung out with a different class of people. You had to be a part of their click for them to like you. So, I didn't get to hang out with her as much as I used to.

After I moved I was still dating the same guy and I would travel back and forth on the weekends to see him. As we used drugs more frequently I started to get bored with the relationship. I was so strung out. So, I wound up cheating on him and when he found out he was livid. He got so mad that he hit me in the face. That was it, I knew that I would put up with some things, but I would never let anyone hit me, so I ended the relationship. We tried to reconnect, but it just didn't work. Even though I was strung out and a mess, I knew that I wasn't going to let anyone physically abuse me. So, I moved on.

I didn't seem to have the redheaded/glasses complex anymore and I slept with whoever I wanted to, and I came and went when I felt like it. If I was mistreated by a man that was it the relationship was over immediately. I was a frosted blonde with contacts. I had my own car, a Camaro and I knew I was hot.

I somehow continued to stay in school and I did well and graduated. I won a monetary gift and received the most improved student award. I celebrated my graduation by walking the High School platform in my white robe and high heels. I received my diploma which filled me with great happiness followed by lots of alcohol. We held a graduation party at my house for some of my friends and of course ex-boyfriends. I managed to stay friends with them. After my party then I continued to other people's parties. The last thing I recall from High school is hearing my one teacher say, "one day we will read about you in the newspapers". I just laughed. I never quite knew what that meant until years later.

In the upcoming chapters, you'll understand what my teacher meant. My mother and first stepfather decided to give it another go at being together. I was so happy. In my mind things seemed like they were getting better. This was the end of my school years. I had to decide what I wanted to do now that I was becoming an adult and I knew that I didn't want to go to college. I had enough of school already and I barely made it through twelfth grade. I was grateful for my parents because I appreciated their trust in me to decide what my next move was.

I had an opportunity to travel to California with my friend and so that is what I chose to do next and they agreed. It was only supposed to be a short trip. I wound up staying there longer than expected and during my absence my mother and stepfather had called it quits for good. That made me sad.

I had no prior obligations to meet after graduating so going to California seemed like a dream come true. My friend and I took a five-day bus ride on a Greyhound bus to California. We washed up in the bathroom sinks and changed our clothes often to keep from smelling. It was only supposed to be a vacation and a short stay. My friend was a hippie who loved a band called the Grateful Dead. That was one of the main reasons we went to California to see a concert out there. I didn't know we were going to travel like gypsies with the Grateful Dead while they were touring from state to state. We had so much fun but after a while I wasn't enjoying the scene as much as my friend was. I wasn't a true hippie. I just went because she asked me to go with her. I wasn't fond of sleeping outside with no bed in the cold with strangers. We were running out of money and couldn't afford hotels anymore, so we had to start hanging out overnight at the stadiums where everyone was partying all night long. I was getting tired of it. I was cold and hungry often.

We would hook up with different people and hang out in their hotel rooms. I was left with some creepy people and at times couldn't find my friend. Eventually she wound up showing up and we left the weirdos behind. I started partying with other people in bars and would go home with strangers. One night I woke up in a motel all by myself and then I remembered that I got sick and vomited all over the place and the guy left me there. I had no idea where I was, and I had no money. I wound up taking a bus back to where my friend was.

After living this way for a while I met this guy who was a hippie. I had never met him before in my life. Our paths crossed by me associating with strangers who would gather together and party in a motel room or over someone's house. He just so happened to be at one of these parties. I wound up separating from my friend and was hanging out with this guy instead. We would sleep outside often, stay at shelters, sleep on the top of mountains and eventually we lived in his car. Being with a guy was more fun than being with my friend.

For food, we ate veggies out of a can and went to the local Salvation Army for dinner. We eventually met up with these Indians at a Grateful Dead concert. They were selling food out of their business truck. They took us home with them and allowed us to live out of a garage that they owned. They would feed us miracle whip sandwich spread on bread to eat most days. We slept on this tiny twin mattress on the floor inside their garage. We both finally got jobs by befriending the Indian people and we worked for them selling jewelry. My boyfriend didn't care for the Indian guy because he knew that he liked me, but he was helping us out, so he put up with him.

Eventually I became a taxi cab driver for the Indian's cab company. I had no clue where I was driving to or how to get around the city. I just used common sense to figure it out. Mostly, I'd pick up people at the racetrack and that is where I made most of my money. We were then able to eat at a pizzeria called Blondies instead of always eating sandwiches with spread on it. It was so much better having money! We eventually got kicked out of the garage because the neighbors saw that we were living there, and they didn't like it.

I was still using drugs and drinking heavily. I mean what else did I have to do? My boyfriend and I was not getting along as well as we use to. I don't know if it was the stress of the way we were living or what. I was driving the cab, so I could get money up for airfare to get back home. We were breaking up so to speak. One night the Indian guy invited me to have some drinks with him and his friend. I trusted him, so I went. We were in a VW bus and we were drinking a lot. I have no idea till this day what they gave me. I just knew I was getting incapacitated quickly. I wasn't afraid of the Indian guy because he never did anything to make me afraid of him. He was a married man with a child and he seemed harmless. After we all started to get drunk the two men started to take advantage of me. I wasn't sure what was happening at first until I realized there were two men touching me everywhere, so I yelled repeatedly no and for them to stop! So, they did.

When I finally reached my boyfriend on the phone to tell him what had happened to me he was so mad that he was crying. He could not believe that they did this to me and he took me home. I finally got my plane ticket and we both went back to NJ. When we arrived back home we visited with our families and friends and then got ready to go back to California but to a different area. We decided to stay together. We wanted to live in Hollywood this time. My boyfriend received a car from a family member and we used that as our transportation to get back to California.

That car turned out to be our source for everything, driving, sleeping, sex, storage, you name it. It was packed with all our stuff. We used to sleep on top of the bags of clothes that were piled up in the back seat. We had to find new parking spots every three days to sleep in, so the police didn't tow the car away. Our relationship was never built on love at first sight. We kind of grew to love each other. At times, the relationship was very strained, but we decided to stay together and get an apartment in California.

I was now officially twenty-one. I started to waitress at Denny's while he was doing telemarketing. We lived a few blocks from Hollywood Blvd. It was an exciting place to live at our age. There was always some kind of action happening. Things were going okay between us because we didn't see each other often. I was still drinking heavily. I was also making good money and was taking care of most of the bills and food. I think that bothered him that I made more money than he did. I could feel us starting to separate. We would fight more often than we used to. We would have bad fights to where I would kick the door in because he would lock me out. When that happened, I would go and stay upstairs with our lesbian friends just to keep the peace. They loved having me anyway. It made me even sadder that this was happening to us and it made me drink even more. He wanted his independence and he wanted me at the same time and that wasn't going to work with me. He had the attitude of I have a girlfriend, but I am not quite taken once we broke up and got back together. He still wanted to live the hippie lifestyle. I was a rocker chick which was the opposite of the hippie lifestyle. So, our differences got in the way.

We moved around a couple of times during our relationship but then split up in California. I went to live with my girlfriend and he started to date other people. I was with a few different people myself. During our separation, my ex and I started talking again and decided that we wanted to get back together and this time we moved to another state. His parents lived out there, so I thought maybe it would be a good thing. I knew before moving that we had to stay with his parents for a while before moving into our own home. I was okay with the idea until I started living with them.

He was not on the best terms with his parents which didn't help the situation. They weren't too fond of his hippie lifestyle or with the fact that he was bringing a girl back home. They were more reserved. It was difficult for me living there because I had to sleep in a separate bed from him. I was a vegetarian which his mother wasn't happy about. I heard her say that I had to eat whatever she makes which I thought was so rude. So, I would skip dinners with them and instead go ride my bike until it was time to go to bed. It was like walking on eggshells while living there.

We finally met some friends which gave us an outlet of some kind. Another place to go instead of sitting in his parents' house all the time. Our new friend who was wheel chair bound would invite us over to his place often. We used to do a lot of drugs with this guy. Eventually we got jobs and had enough money to move into our own place which we were so excited about. We even got ourselves a dog.

We moved into our new place and furnished it. We even had our friends come over and celebrate with us the day we moved in. We had jobs, a new home and everything seemed to be falling into place. It was nice to finally seem like we were having a family like atmosphere going on. I was ready to commit to him and move forward but he wasn't. I found out a little while later that my boyfriend was still calling his ex-girlfriends and chatting with them often. This so hurt me especially since we were back together and trying to make things work. I just couldn't stand it anymore. We had one last major fight about the conversations he had with other women and him not wanting to give that up. For me that was the last straw. That night I went to bed and the next morning I wound up packing all my things into my car and I headed back to NJ. I received one last phone call from him when I had arrived in NJ asking if I had made it home safely and I never talked with him again until years later.

I had no place to call my own in NJ. My mother was already living with her boyfriend and my other family members had no room. My aunt was gracious enough to welcome me into her small place with her two kids and her husband. I lived there for a while until I got a job and moved in with my new roommate. I started to date a bunch of different men because I didn't want a boyfriend. I had enough of men abusing me and using me for a while. I was just happy being single and going out to bars with my girlfriends. I had friends who were strippers and friends who were married and who cheated on their husbands and I didn't care. I had no moral ethics at this point. I had enough of my own disappointments to deal with. I didn't want to get involved in anyone else's mess.

I was dating men that were younger than me and men that were older than me. From Police officers to bar owners, restaurant owners, it didn't matter. I had access to anything I wanted from money to drugs, food, and plenty of gifts from men. I decided I didn't need to be tied down to one man anyhow because all they do is break your heart. I figured I will be the one who will break hearts now. My new roommate and I got along great because she was a worse alcoholic than I was. Her and her boyfriend was a mess. I rarely ever stayed in our apartment because it was extremely small. Not to mention she always had her boyfriend over. When I was home it was just to sleep there or to bring men home to have sex for the night.

I was getting involved deeply into cocaine at this point and I was drinking every night. I went to work to make money so that I could budget for my bills and rent. The rest would be spent on alcohol and drugs. I could drink men under the table. I would stay out until the bars closed and then go to an afterhours place to drink some more and then after that to some one's house to drink even more. I would wake up in stranger's homes because I would go there to party. At times, I didn't even know what town I was in when I woke up the next morning. I would forget where I parked my car. It was a reckless lifestyle that I was leading. It's no wonder I never overdosed or had to be hospitalized from alcohol poisoning or wound up dead somewhere.

Lesson Learned: Although I had a wonderful opportunity to travel and experience new things I took it a little too far. How many know that we can go to extremes sometimes in a whole other direction when we don't have to. I stayed in a place with people that I had no reason to be with. It did take me through a journey that forever changed the course of my life. I know that the enemy of my soul was trying to make sure that I would never reach the full potential that my life had to offer. I thank God that I am much wiser now in my older years. I can say that as I look back I have learned a great wealth of information to share with others. I learned that in life we need to appreciate the little things, such as food, clothing, and shelter. I lived out on the streets and I learned how to survive without money. I learned that I had to rely on other people to feed and clothe me through donations and charity. I pan handled for my food. Now I'm not blaming anyone for the lifestyle that I was leading because I chose to live that way. No one forced me to live like that. I must say I did enjoy not having to work or pay bills and that living on the streets was easier than being responsible but the price you must pay is not worth it. Like being touched by older men or abused along the way. Like not getting justice because you're just a homeless person. I suffered from scabies because I put on dirty clothing from a charity. I chose to sleep outside and use the restrooms in public parks and gas stations. It wasn't a pretty lifestyle, but it was the one I was living. I had never lived this way before. I was a whole different person. I just didn't care anymore about myself. And although I was blessed to visit the many states along my travels the thing I remember the most about this journey was that as I look back I know there was a God watching over this once little seven-year-old who used to pray for His protection and love and who allowed me to make it through this season of life safely. I learned what it was like to have no money and to be hungry. I felt what it was like to be cold, wet, and dirty. I know what compassion is now more than ever. I ate in the parks where people would graciously come to feed the homeless and the poor because I was one of them. I can relate to how it feels to stay in shelters and how it feels to lack the necessities of life. I understand what it is to be mindful of the things I do have and to be grateful instead of complaining about the things I don't have. I know that I have a God that supplies all my needs. Even when I wasn't acknowledging Him. He did it when I was living on the streets. I learned that alcohol and drugs do not have to rule my life and it isn't the way I have to live. I learned that even though I was hurt so many times by different men that it doesn't mean that all men are going to be the same way towards me. I have learned what real love is and that it was not about me giving away my virginity to a man. I know that no man has the right to touch me when I say no. I have learned that life can steer you in the wrong direction but if you are in the right mindset you can always make a U-turn! It is never too late to make changes. Change is good! I liken it to when the caterpillar thinks that life is ending while being in the cocoon. Everything is claustrophobic and bound by limitations. When suddenly a metamorphosis starts taking place and a whole new atmosphere is being birthed and is manifesting into this new creation. A miracle at new life is creating itself from the inside. It's then that it suddenly breaks free without warning and it becomes something so much more beautiful than it originally was. We have the same opportunity to change. I don't look at people the same way anymore now that I have lived this lifestyle for myself. If tomorrow never came what would you regret today that you haven't done yet? Experience life, the good, the bad and the ugly. Put your experiences under the "lessons" file. Use those experiences to build upon. Use them to teach others. Use them to better yourself! Make sure you understand the choices your making and why you're making them. Let these choices add to your life not subtract from it. If your questioning a certain area in your life then sit down with yourself and pray about it, write it out, speak to yourself about it and don't rush to get an answer. Let it all simmer until it feels peaceful. Don't look at the things that seem like they're not panning out in life as failures there is no such thing, they are learning curves. What are you learning right now from your experiences, what are you teaching yourself? Are you stirring up your passions, are you being your own cheerleader? Get in the game. It's time to rise to the occasion of your life! The only dreams that die are the ones that you give up on. Write the vision and make it plain and then run with it so that others may see it. It's your time to shine!

Ephesians 3:20 – Now all glory to God, who is able, through His mighty power at work within us, to accomplish infinitely more than we might ask or think.

Chapter 4- Sexual Addictions

My very first encounter with witnessing sex was when I was seven years old. It happened by accident. It was in my home. I had to use the bathroom in the middle of the night. So, I jumped out of bed and headed there. The only way to get to the bathroom was through my parent's room. It was dark and quiet for a moment until I reached their bedroom door. What my eyes saw next did not look anything like I had ever seen before! I had no clue what was happening between them. By the sounds and movements that I heard I thought that my step father was hurting my mom. I quickly ran back into my room with tears streaming down my face and shut my bedroom door. My parents were having sex! Thank God, they never knew I was there to witness such an event.

Now, let's get back to me being all grown up and an adult who was living on my own. I had different types of friends, some of them happened to be strippers and so I started to hang out with them more because they always liked to go to the bars. I was what you called a total bar hopper by now. The bars were a familiar atmosphere to me because that's the environment I grew up in. So, it only made sense that I would follow in that vein. I was ingesting so much alcohol at this point that I could out drink half of the men in the bar. I had no shame in doing so and I was proud of it like I was a pro.

At the bars, my friends and I would often pick up strangers and go home with them. I was a woman who got what she wanted even if it was another woman's man! I had a lot of confidence, but I used it in the wrong areas of my life. My habits were out of control and so was my sex life. You read about how I lost my virginity in the previous chapter and I hated it but when I got used to having sex I fell in love with the act. So much so that my friend and I used to bet on who we would go home with from the bar by the end of the night. We would pick a man out and by the end of the night, nine times out of ten we hooked up with that man.

My friend and I had a system. If a guy approached either one of us at a bar or party and we weren't interested in him then we would act like lesbians and start kissing each other. When we were interested in the guy then we would separate ourselves, so he knew we were straight. There were many times when I would wake up in a stranger's house and not even remember what happened the night before. I would forget that my friend took my car home and I would think that my car was stolen. That's how out of control I was with my drinking.

As if that wasn't bad enough, when I got very drunk I would get lost while driving somewhere. One time I was so drunk that it took me an hour to get to my boyfriend's house which typically only took twenty minutes. I was so drunk that I couldn't remember how to get there. When I got to his home I proceeded to drink even more by going to another bar. I didn't know when to quit. I was so plastered that I was falling off the bar stool. The bartender told my boyfriend that he needed to take me home. That was a nice way to say, get her out of here! As I left the bar I laid down outside on the cement and was unable to walk. My boyfriend had to take me home to his place.

After that episode finally ended and I slept through my hangover I got into my car to go back home. When I got inside my car I found hair stuck in my visor. I thought what did I do last night? All I can say is scary! You think that would have stopped me, right? Wrong!

I never thought at the time that I had any sexual addictions or an alcohol problem. I just thought it was normal to want sex all the time and to drink every night. I didn't know any better because I grew up around this stuff.

The bar scene became my second home. I was there more than I was at my own apartment. The only time I went home was to shower, sleep and change clothes. I had my favorite spots that my friend and I liked to go to. People knew us well. We never had a problem making friends. We had people who would buy our drinks for us or who would share their drugs. There was never a time or place that we couldn't go to and get high. There was never a shortage of men either.

Concerning my sexual orientation, I had dabbled and kissed other women, but I loved men. I had a deep desire to have sex all the time. It got so bad that when I wasn't with a sexual partner I had to use other means to satisfy my flesh. I did this because when I didn't have a man to have sex with, I needed to satisfy my sexual lusts. They had grown so out of control along with my drinking. I went through a stage of having sex all the time. I had it as much as I could because it was fulfilling a need. A need that I did not know I had to fill.

Do you know how women prostitute for sex? I was doing it for free. No charge! I was just giving my body away. Most of the time I chose the man that I wanted to have sex with so in my mind I guess I thought I was in control of the situation. But, there were times I had men tell me that I was too drunk to do anything with them and I would just pass out and they would leave. But I would still attempt to have sex no matter how drunk I was.

It wasn't about love, remember I couldn't care less about love! I can't say that I understood why I had these compulsions. Except for the fact that not one relationship that I was ever in worked out up until this point. No one showed me what real love looked like. So, to have sex without being in a relationship didn't hurt, because there was no connection anyhow. I didn't have to feel anything after one night with a man if I didn't want to. It was the easy way out. It wasn't hard for me to pick up men. Since I had changed a lot by this time. I was better looking with a great figure. I could command the attention of any man. Men finally wanted me for a change. The problem for some of the men that I would have sex with was that I would now break their hearts because I didn't want to commit. How could I? I wasn't even committed to myself. Broken people can't help other broken people. I was so deceived, but I thought I was living a good life, the satisfying life. The truth was that I was never being fulfilled because the need was always haunting me. I wanted to know what real love was but became too afraid to find it.

Another problem that developed with me was that when I didn't go home with a guy because it was a weeknight and the bars were kind of slow, I'd always have a back-up guy to go home with. As much as I thought I was an independent person I was very co-dependent on a man for sex. I would always hook up with this one guy. It was strictly to party and have sex and nothing else. It was like an unspoken rule between us. The thought of us ever becoming boyfriend and girlfriend never crossed our minds! We knew that we weren't the perfect fit and that we would never fall in love and marry. It just wasn't that way between us. He was left on reserve for the lonely nights and that was it. He liked someone else that I knew, and I was fine with that.

I didn't have a preference of the type of men that I would have sex with. I would be with men who were married and who were divorced. Some of them had girlfriends. Yet they would show up at my house to take me out and have sex. I had one man who wanted to leave his wife for me. I stole a man from the woman he was with for three years because I wanted him and guess what, he left her for me. I would show up in the same place where she would be, and she had no idea he was sleeping with me. I was getting to the point where I wanted to incorporate other sexual activities into my routine. I would have sex with men and boyfriends in the oddest of places. I have had sex in cars, outside, in bathrooms on top of bars and restaurant tables. On pool tables, in the ocean, swimming pools, hotels, and motels, with other people in the same room, you name it I probably had sex there.

Some scary things have happened to me because of alcohol, drugs, and sexual addictions. It's no joke when you are not functioning in the right mindset. You will tend to do anything. One night like I often did, I went to a bar. I was in a bar that I was not familiar with. I met up with a guy in the bar and he invited me to his apartment to party after hours. He lived above the bar. When the bar closed, I went upstairs with the guy. We smoked weed, drank some more, and chatted but I did not have sex with him. Which was extremely unusual. When I woke up the next morning in his apartment he told me that I had passed out. Then the guy had discussed with me that he was glad that I passed out and that I didn't have sex with him. He went on to tell me that he had HIV. I was like what? I quickly thanked him for a good time and left as soon as I could. I know that God was with me, it sounds crazy but remember as a little girl I used to pray for Him to be near me always? God answers us when we don't even realize it.

I will leave you with this last very scary episode due to my addictions. When I lived in California I use to visit the Rainbow Bar. On this night, I decided to stay at the bar without my friends. I was toxic with alcohol by the time the bar closed. I was so drunk that I figured I better get home. I hopped into a cab and suddenly a man hopped in on the other side of me. He asked me if I wouldn't mind sharing the cab with him. Back then I didn't think about murderers or rapists, so I wasn't concerned with this guy. Before long he had conned me into going back to his place to party. He said he had alcohol. Now, all the bars were closing and there was no place to buy any alcohol, so I said why not. We arrived at a motel and he asked me to come inside. I thought this was a joke, but he said he lived there. So, I went in. There was nothing but trash in an empty room with a phone in the middle of the floor. He had no furniture either. He had lied about having a bunch of alcohol and had only one beer left in his refrigerator, so he offered it to me. At this point I was disappointed. He wasn't an ugly guy, but I was looking forward to a couple more drinks otherwise I could have just gone home. I was drunk enough.

He just wanted sex. He knew that I was drunk enough to bring to his so-called home and he took the opportunity to do so. Even though I was very drunk for some reason the funniest thing happened, I would not have sex with him. This was not like me. I don't even know why I declined. I allowed other things to happen but not sex. The following morning, I woke up and realized that something was wrong with this scene. It was so frightening to be in a hotel room with a stranger who had no furniture except a phone which he was talking on when I awoke.

We had slept on the floor because there was no bed or couch. I was nervous because I had no idea where I was or in what town I was in. When I woke up he was talking to someone on the phone about drugs as if he needed them. He was a junkie. I had to call my friend and ask her how to get back to her place where I was staying. After realizing that I didn't have sex with this guy I was so relieved because once again I was protected this time from a junkie. Who knows what I would have caught from him. Years later when I was watching the news they showed a man whose name was Richard Ramirez. He was a satanist and was charged with murder. After seeing his picture, I was then brought back to the memory of the man that I was in the hotel room with who was a junkie that looked just like this Richard guy. I will never forget that moment. I cannot say for sure that it was him that I was with in that hotel room, but I cannot deny that it wasn't him either. Another God intervention over my life.

So, after going back and forth between California and Florida I finally moved back to NJ. When I got back to my home state I moved into a place with a roommate who I found through the newspaper. We got along well because we were both alcoholics. We were always getting drunk or high and she never minded that I brought home strange men.

I was in my own messed up reality, yet I thought I was a strong self-sufficient woman. I worked. I paid the rent and my bills all on my own and on time. I didn't owe anyone a thing. No one had control over me. The problem with that is you can have all your ducks in a row on the outside and, yet the inside looks like a Mack truck hit you. On the inside, I was void of the proper affection. I used men, alcohol, and drugs to love me instead of loving myself. All those things took the place of me being who God created me to be. I didn't know my identity. My identity was always being made fun of or rejected by others. So, at an early age I decided to try and become someone else! It wasn't the real me and because I wasn't authentic nothing around me was either. There was no stability or trust. It wasn't until I found out who I was that I realized that I didn't need sex, alcohol, or drugs to feel loved anymore. These things did not do one thing to fill the void in my heart. They led me further away from God.

I had forgotten about God! The only time that I ever remembered God since I was that little girl in her room praying was when I thought I was pregnant. I would pray to God because I knew somehow that He would listen to me when I was in trouble. Isn't that what we're taught? Run to God when you're in trouble. Guess what I found out? He is so much more than that kind of God and when I found out who He was instead of who I thought He might be, it was only then that I found myself and my real identity.

Let me share with you an incident that happened to me, so you'll know that God doesn't forget your cries for help, ever! Even in our darkest moments He knows how bad you need Him. One day I was extremely hung over and had fallen asleep on the couch from the night before. I slept into the mid- afternoon so that I could rest up for that evening. There was no darkness surrounding me only light because it was daytime. Suddenly, I was awoken from my sleep and when I opened my eyes I saw a man who was extremely calm just sitting on the edge of the couch staring at me with great love. I got so scared because I knew I wasn't dreaming. My eyes were physically open looking at a stranger sitting next to me. I immediately shut my eyes again and then very quickly opened them and He was gone.

He was so calm and never reacted to me being scared. He never said one word to me. He had on a short camel colored robe with a rope like belt. He looked almost like a pauper, yet he was perfect looking. He seemed like an ordinary man but with great authority. He was very meek. He had brown wavy hair that parted in the middle and it came to the top of His shoulders. He was wearing brown sandals. He was in a sitting position with his leg lifted over the other as a man would cross his legs. He had his head resting in His hand as He just watched me. Then He disappeared. Everything about Him exuded peace. Not until many years later did I realized that this man was Jesus and He was visiting me in my darkest times.

I know Jesus usually appears in His white robe most of the time, but He can appear as anything He likes. I believe He came to me in this form because He wanted me to remember this encounter that I had with Him. That it was real and not a dream. That I knew that He personally came to Earth in human form to visit me. I believe He didn't want me to think it was some form of delusion from my drinking if He came another way. I knew this man looking at me was not just any ordinary man. It was someone in the spirit realm that was looking at me and then He disappeared, and He put me right back to sleep in perfect peace. Something transpired during His visit with me, but it didn't manifest in my life right then.

Years later when I had realized that it was Jesus who was sitting on the end of my couch watching over me I understood why He made that type of appearance to me. It was so that I could look back on that day and say that God was always with me and has never left my side.

Regarding my promiscuity, I know that God had protected me even in my chaotic season because I never wound up with any deadly diseases or HIV/Aids regardless of how many times I had unprotected sex. I teetered with bi-sexual tendencies, but it was more out of curiosity than considering it. I didn't understand myself. So, I was re-inventing a different person. I was trying other avenues to see where I truly lived in my heart. I thought I could like that alter ego or the double minded person better. That was a lie and so far from the truth.

We as humans are looking to satisfy the lusts of our bodies because our hearts are void of genuine love. So, what happens is we surrender ourselves to destructive ways because of the sufferings that are going on internally inside of us. Whatever they may be, rejection, self-hatred, being raped, or being sexually or mentally abused, unwanted, or unloved. We want a way of escape and it is in these moments of escape that the enemy of our soul seeks the gratification of our demise.

The character assassination of who we were truly meant to be which is in the likeness of God our creator is at stake every time we treat ourselves in this manner. These weak moments cause us to take the road that is headed for a dead end. When the issues in our lives are not handled properly they show up in other ways. They are self-destructive and can even be deadly. Most of the time we don't even recognize that it's happening to us.

Lesson Learned: It's important who you surround yourself with. It's also important to evaluate yourself or ask someone outside of your sphere to tell you how they see you. An outside opinion that you can trust may be needed. If you find that you can't go a day, week, or month without something, you just may have an addiction. Promiscuity, alcohol, or drugs should not be your 1st love or the love of your life. These things do not bring any fruit or happiness to the table. In my experience, I know that they don't benefit your life or anyone else's. Remember, the enemy of your soul has a plan to steal your identity. He will continue to steal for as long as he can until you come unto the realization of who you were created to be. He will try to take you off the plan of destiny to the land of the lost. The enemy never wants you to be well, competent, and loved. Love is so pure when it's genuine. It's not rude, proud, it doesn't lie, hide, cheat, steal, boast nor is it selfish. The enemy is! So, if you see some of these things starting to rule over your flesh and soul you should recognize that it's not a part of Gods plan for your life. God is love, and He doesn't display Himself in negative ways that bring destruction to your life. He will even show up at times even if you don't know it. Just keep your eyes open and stay positive about the problem because you're never alone. You have the power to transform any trial into a victory. I believe in you! As far as sex, it belongs in the bedroom! Don't disrespect your body, character, or intelligence by putting yourself in atmospheres that could lead you down a wrong path. It's down these paths that lead to roads that become wider opportunities for darkness to creep in. With this darkness comes with it all the unknowns that could be detrimental to your life. Things like rape, contracting deadly diseases and unwanted pregnancies. It may even lead to death. Value yourself! Your worth more than a few fleeting thoughts and one-night stands from some misguided advice from strangers. Forgiveness is so powerful. It's meant for the person needing healing not the betrayer. The betrayer must find their own path. For you, you must heal. Know that these one-night stands, or a night of drinking, is not how you want to explain to your future children how they got here. They'll think they were a mistake subconsciously. There's no condemnation for those that this has happened to because I'm one of those people. What I have experienced is that having children in a marriage setting has its own spiritual blessings to it. So, forgive yourself if your caught up in any of these types of situations. Recognition is the key to knowing there could be a problem. This is the first step to your recovery. Once this happens then the chains that bind your heart will be released and you'll be free to be who God created you to truly be. Your inner-self will begin to flourish. You'll be able to find your way onto the paths of blessings and fruitfulness that will fill your life up to abundance and overflow. You'll be a happier you! All those dreams that were on hold can still be lived. It's never too late to bring them to pass. Your reality will bring focus and attract good things to your life. It's so worth it. Take my word for it! Remember to take care of your body. It's a temple. It houses so many valuable things. Your hidden parts are not for sale or to be used for free. Sexual partners aren't the answer either. What they are, are compensations for other needs that must be filled. Your body understands the trauma that you put it through. So be kind to it. Honor it. Love yourself! Be free to be you. Remember it's okay to say No!

Psalm 84:11 – For the Lord God is our sun and our shield. He gives us grace and glory. The Lord will withhold no good thing from those who do what is right.

Chapter 5-The Abortion

When I returned to NJ I started working as a waitress. I had no experience in any other field of work where I could make fast money. I needed money daily, so I could feed my drinking habit. As I already mentioned I finally found a roommate and we shared her apartment. I could freely come and go as I please. At the restaurant where I worked I became friends with a few of the other waitresses there. I found out that they were heavily into cocaine like I was. I found myself living off this drug daily. I would stay up all night drinking in the bars until closing time. Then go to an afterhours bar. Then I'd sleep all day and wake up to do cocaine and alcohol all over again. It was the same routine day after day.

While working at the restaurant I met this guy who was one of the head chefs. He started conversing with me a lot. Then the flirting started. I found myself liking him too. One thing led to another and we started to hang out together. After work, we would meet up at the bar where me and the girls used to go to drink. Then when the bar closed he and I would go back to my house to have sex. This was another relationship that never grew into a boyfriend and girlfriend status, but everyone knew we were sleeping together. It was against the rules to date in the work place. So, we had to pretend we didn't know each other that well so that we didn't get fired. Which was hard for me because I started to care about him.

I was getting my periods regularly. There were no worries until one month came and went by without any sign of it. Then I got scared! I have never told any of my family members except for one person about what I am about to publicly share with you. I was pregnant! When the test came back positive I was speechless. I didn't know what to do because I had never been in this situation before, ever! The first thing that I did was confront the father about the pregnancy. I never thought I would hear the words that I heard him say to me. He told me that he didn't want anything to do with a baby or me and he asked me to come by his apartment to pick up money to get the abortion over with. I never talked to him again.

I thought why is this happening now? I had just turned twenty-one years old and I was legally allowed to drink. I was at the peak of my adulthood. Then my whole world came to a crashing halt. All kinds of thoughts were spinning around in my head as I asked myself what am I going to do now?

The next thing I did was go to my best friend. When I told her that I was pregnant, and the father wanted nothing to do with the pregnancy she was all for raising my child. She was against abortion. I was so in awe that she would even offer to do that I was in tears. She was a cocaine addict and worse than me. She was not an option for my situation and I felt very lonely. When the father of our baby told me that he did not want anything to do with me, I felt that my decision had already been made. All kinds of emotions started to fill my brain and I was a mess.

In my mind, I felt that I was not meant to be a mother at the time. I had convinced myself of that. I was inexperienced. I just moved into my very own place. I had just turned twenty-one and honestly, I was not in any shape to be a mom. I was an alcoholic and a drug addict. I felt like I had just reached a pinnacle in my independence and that I was not even close to thinking about motherhood. I couldn't even picture it. I didn't even want relationships with other men, let alone a baby.

I lived in a tiny apartment with a roommate who was also an alcoholic and whose boyfriend practically lived with us. There was not any more room in that tiny apartment for one more person. I also rationed in my mind that I would not be able to provide financially for the both of us and that I had no one outside of my roommate that I could live with. It seemed that my list of reasons to have the abortion got longer than a "yes" list to have a baby. I was so torn and crushed. I did not believe in God the way I do now and so having an abortion became what seemed like the only choice for me. I felt that with no support and the fact that I was so young did not qualify me to be a parent. I felt helpless and empty. I also felt that although my mother and I were close there was no way I could share this with her because she would be crushed. That was the last thing I wanted to do to her. There was only one person that I could trust and that was my cousin.

The one who I felt was like a sister to me while we were growing up. She was the only one who knew about my dilemma and she was so gracious to me by not saying anything critical about my decision, she just did what I asked without many questions. I was so grateful that she was there in my time of need and available to help me. No one else knew what was happening and I asked her not to tell another soul. I recall the drive over the bridge into Philadelphia as my eyes scanned every tall industrial building in the hopes of taking my mind off what lied ahead. My cousin had borrowed her mother's car and she was familiar with Philadelphia, so she knew where to go. I remember approaching the clinic with uncertainty and a feeling that I had never felt before of the struggle that was going on in my heart. I had believed that I was doing the right thing in my mind, but my heart was screaming out for justice over the situation to keep this baby. I was extremely scared and sad at the same time.

I recall a person calling me into a room after I had checked into the abortion clinic and she started to explain all my options. She then told me about the procedure and what would happen afterwards. The worst feeling of all was when I was taken to the room which was very tiny and cold. I was told to undress from the waist down and to lay on the table and someone would be with me shortly. I was about eight weeks pregnant per their estimation. I found out at about four to five weeks when I missed my period and then had to schedule the abortion which brought me to eight weeks at the termination. I remember laying on that cold table and a man walking into the room silently. I don't recall seeing his face as if he was invisible. He never said a word to me.

Suddenly my feet were in stir-ups and a clamp was inserted to open my womb. I then heard a suctioning sound which was very loud. I felt intense cramping and I became nauseated. I told the lady who stood beside me that I was sick, and she immediately got me a plastic nausea bin just in case. The procedure went quickly and before I knew it was over. I would be lying if I said it wasn't painful because it was! My insides and a tiny human being where being sucked out of me for God sake.

I was then escorted out of that room into a waiting room with about five to six other pregnant women who were waiting or who had already been taken care of. I remember seeing a woman who was about five to six months pregnant and I couldn't understand how she could be having an abortion. I just knew this whole thing was wrong.

When it was over, I was so sick that I immediately ran to the bathroom and I could not stop vomiting. When I returned to the resting room they told me to lie down and they gave me Tylenol. Right away they started talking to me about birth control. I couldn't believe it!

When I left the clinic, I felt so empty inside. I cried and cried as the emptiness from within my heart and body was now void of any form of life inside of me. Apart of me had been torn from my own body and I knew it was never going to come back.

The pain in my uterus was intense and it kept bringing me constant reminders of what could have been. My cousin drove us home. I immediately just wanted to go into a dark room and remain alone in silence to sleep and rest my weary body. I went into my cousin's room and I stayed there all day and night.

I know now that the baby that I aborted is in Heaven awaiting my arrival one day and I can't wait to see her or him. I hope it's a girl because I never had any girls. I asked God to forgive me for the act that I committed against his creation in my life and I know He has. If I had the faith that I have now I would have never made that decision. I was under the notion that a baby was not a person until up to three or four months of pregnancy and that what was growing inside of me was just tissue that was forming. That was what they taught us.

When I was better, the next day I quit work, so I wouldn't have to see the father of our aborted baby ever again. I didn't see him until a couple of months later. He was with his new girlfriend who had once been my friend from work and he wound up getting her pregnant next and they decided to keep the baby. That hurt. It was another big let-down concerning men for me. This was the real kicker and it changed my life.

Lesson Learned: Life is a gift! Yet, things will happen in our lives and those things that occur will not always be a bed of roses or ideal situations. We all face those choices that we wish someone else had to deal with instead of us. God created humans and gave them the freedom to do with their lives what they will. Every day we get a chance to make good choices. What we do with these choices will be determined by the type of outcome that results from what we chose. Choices can cause us to flourish or become stagnant. Excel or be defeated. The mind is a powerful tool to help us navigate through life's obstacles. Although most people don't sit around thinking about how many bad choices they're going to make, it still happens. The reason we may make bad decisions are because of root causes with in our souls. Due to some form of trauma or neglect at some point in our lives. There are several factors that could be the culprit to making such bad choices. Things like ignorance or being uneducated. Adultery, divorce, loss of a loved one. Rejection, grief, addictions, molestation, and the list goes on. Let's be real, bad things happen to good people. The key is not to act on a bad choice from the brokenness in our lives. Did you ever hear the phrase "tomorrow is not promised?" It's true for all of us. What we must do in the meantime is occupy until they come so to speak. Who are they? The people that we want in our lives and our inner circle of friends. The ones who are supporters and who bring a positive vibe to our lives. If we remain broken and negative in our choices, we'll never get to experience the good things life offers us. They say we become like the environment that we're around. So, to do good, we must know better. Some of us must learn how to make better choices. For me I didn't have the support, the education, or the stability that I needed to make the right choice concerning my abortion. I should have taken the time and sought out people who could have helped me and educated me more on the facts. Instead I took the negative approach and let fear, rejection and my emotions creep into my thoughts and I made decisions based off lies. What I've learned is that where there is a problem there is a solution. Today I understand who God is and how He has given us the world so that we can seize opportunities from it so that we can decide to be whole from the inside out. We don't have to stay broken forever. Life is not without its struggles, but a life based on good choices makes the journey so much better. We should never give into impossibilities or think that there are no answers to our problems. Just because we haven't been informed properly the first time does not mean we cannot have a do over. God is the God of love. When I understood that He loved me, my broken pieces started to mend. I started to make better choices. God can cause you to become a new creation. Old things pass away, and you can become a new you! He will help you to develop a new mindset too. When I discovered these things about God I found out that I didn't have to carry around all the shame and guilt that I was carrying around with me anymore. I knew that He had forgiven me because I asked Him to. The great thing about God is that He understands our frailties and He can relate to our human weaknesses. He also trusts that one day we will learn from our past mistakes. We will gain the wisdom to help others in the process. Like the wisdom, I gained through my abortion. I found out that there is so much help available these days. Adoption is another option. There are clinics that will give you options instead of leading you to choose an abortion. The main thing I learned is honesty. The truth will set you free every time. People may not like to hear it, but it gives them a chance to decide to get help if they choose to. The possibilities are endless. Never put yourself in a position where you compromise your integrity. Your life and the unborn child's life is important. They become someone too! We all matter. Life is so precious! The enemy not only wants to destroy your life but the life of the unborn so that they never reach their destiny either. We can change that! So, remember condemnation is not from God and for every problem you can derive a solution.

Whether it's the perfect solution or not you can still make a good decision by seeking out the truth of the matter. Live and learn! Then you'll do better every time.

Matthew 7:7 – Keep on asking, and you will receive what you ask for. Keep on seeking, and you will find. Keep on knocking, and the door will be opened to you.

Chapter 6- Broken Relationships
(a never-ending saga)

After that chapter of my life was over I began to hang out with a whole different group of people. They were not associated with the previous group that my ex and I hung out with. Within this new group, I met a girl through a mutual friend and we clicked immediately. We hung out with each other practically every day. We did everything together so much so that we even dated guys who were brothers at the same time. I was finally off cocaine at this point in my life. This was a miracle. I didn't have to go to treatment or rehab and no one had to persuade me to stop using cocaine. I decided to quit the habit on my own because I was tired of feeling sick the next day. That was the case with cocaine but not the liquor. I was still an alcoholic. If I wasn't sleeping or working you could find me at the bar getting drunk.

Remember when I said I would take another woman's man? It was true. I was now dating a musician by luring him from another woman. I knew he had a girlfriend, but I didn't care. I had what he wanted. He had a taste of me and I knew he liked what he had. I allowed him time to cross over to my side and he finally did. We were both serious alcoholics. That's what we had in common. We truly became best friends. I fell madly in love with him. So much so that I let my guard down. Our relationship lasted for three years. He was the only man who I ever considered marrying. Especially since I was not the marrying kind. As you see from my history of men abusing me but there was something different about this guy. As our relationship continued I felt secure enough to want to live with him. I could see myself going the long haul with this guy for once in my life. We got along great and barely ever fought.

I still recall the night that I met him. I can picture the booth inside the bar where I was first introduced to him. After several hours of conversation and many drinks later I went home with him. We became inseparable from that night on. We became like one person. Everywhere he went so did I. I supported his musical career and believed in him. He was a good musician and passionate about his work. Plus, we got to be in bars all the time. This went on for a couple of years and we never pressured one another for anything more than what we already shared in the relationship.

When I lived with my roommate he had a key to my apartment. He would come to my house at any time or hour of the night when he was done playing in the bars. I would either be sleeping or out and he would wait up for me. It seemed logical that moving in together now in our relationship was the right thing to do. My lease was about to expire where I lived, and I was ready to ask him if he wanted to live together. He was already rooming with his brother, but I thought eventually his brother would move out. I don't know if he fully liked the whole idea of me moving in with them both, but he agreed to it. I practically lived at his apartment and vice versa already. He finally agreed, and I moved into their apartment. It was a tiny apartment. So, I had to pack all my extra stuff away and take it to a friend's house. I was so excited because I thought we were going to the next level together. I was in a relationship for once that I was enjoying.

As time went by it turned out that I was wrong about moving in with him. When I started incorporating some of my stuff into his house and hanging pictures on the walls I could feel an uneasiness in the apartment. So, I took my things down. That was the first sign. I started feeling like I was alone in the relationship while living there. There were many nights that I would wait up for him into the early morning hours to come home from playing in the bars. I knew his schedule. I used to attend every one of his gigs but when I moved in with him I figured I'd see him more at home instead of going to all his gigs now. I was still working in NJ and had to travel back and forth to his apartment which took up a lot of time and gas. So, I would just go to his apartment after work and wait for him to come home instead. There were many nights when he didn't come home. This was the second sign.

The patterns of him not coming home or coming in at 5am in the morning started looking familiar to me. I started reminiscing in my mind about how he cheated on his other girlfriend with me. He was starting to exhibit the same habits once again. This gave me a reason to believe that now I might be the girlfriend that is possibly being cheated on this time. My so called mended heart once again started to break so I decided to move out of his apartment and go to a friend's house. It just wasn't working out between us living together. At this point I was ready for more and he wasn't which bothered me. I mean we were together for three years now. Even though he swore to me that he would never cheat on me because he had been cheated on before, I still couldn't help but think he was doing just that. I'm not sure why I believed him when he said he'd never cheat on me because he didn't think twice about cheating on the other woman that I took him away from. Isn't it amazing that as humans we can have such twisted thinking at times and ignore our gut feelings?

Despite the situation between us I still decided to see him because after all I was in love with him and had invested a few years of my life into the relationship. We decided to still see each other while living separate lives but we were both changing. He was trying to get sober and I was drinking more than ever. I was probably the worst person he could have been around. I was not ready to quit drinking. This caused him to lose the fight. He was torn between the two. Alcohol or me. I remember coming home to my place before I moved into his place and he would be waiting there for me being very sober while I traipsed in inebriated. I would be a sloppy mess and he would leave because of it. Many things caused him to fall right back into drinking. Being in the business he was in didn't help either because he had to play in bars. Eventually he started to drink again, and I was glad to have my partner back. So, we continued drinking together.

My birthday quickly approached us. I thought this was it, maybe his heart had changed concerning our relationship status. My friend made a big deal about the present he got me. Once again, I was so excited. I thought after all that we had been through and the fact that we still loved each other so much meant that it was time for him to commit. I thought maybe he did not want to lose me after all. I honestly thought that my present contained an engagement ring.

The box was square like a ring box and he seemed so excited about me opening the box. I guess I thought because we were supposedly committed to only one another for three years that this was going to be the next step for us. I had never brought up marriage before nor did I ask him to get engaged because that just wasn't my place. Although secretly I did long for the day that he would one day propose. I opened my gift and I was so excited that I was shaking, and my heart was pounding. I mean what girl doesn't wait for this day her whole life? I looked down in the box and there staring me in the face was a beautiful ruby anklet.

What??? That was the first thing running through my mind. I wasn't sure how I should act. I felt like my heart just fell out of my chest. I quietly thanked him for the anklet. I was sadly disappointed. Disappointed so much so that it changed my whole perspective regarding our relationship. I felt let down all over again but now it was by the man of my dreams. If he had popped the question I would have ran to the alter in a second. Immediately another thought popped into my mind and that was, look at how far the ankle is from the ring finger! That was it. I had made up my mind at that very moment that I wasn't going to take this relationship seriously anymore. I was back on defensive mode. I shut down and even raised a few walls back up over my heart. I was worn out and tired. I think if we had both sobered up together we would have seen the truth for what it was. We would have realized sooner that we were together just for the sex and alcohol or we would have realized that we had nothing in common at all.

I don't even think he ever noticed how sad I was. My interest in pursuing the relationship was over. I shut down completely. I figured I had put enough time and energy into this relationship already and it's going nowhere. I was done wasting my time. I didn't know if he ever wanted to marry me and I didn't care anymore. I didn't want him or anything else he had to offer me. I still saw him on and off because honestly the sex was the best I ever had. That ended quickly after I started seeing another man that I worked with. Don't get me wrong I wasn't in a hurry to be married but I thought he was the "one" my best friend for life. My dream of finding true love was shattered. I didn't think about getting married at all after this relationship ended. I didn't even believe in it anymore. Any of it!

My inner circle of friends changed once again. I started liking a guy who was a few years younger than me. My co-worker was trying to hook us up for a while and it finally worked because I eventually said yes. She invited us over to her house and we started to date. I didn't want anything serious. He was handsome though. My mother use to say he looked like a Chippendale. I was now seeing my previous boyfriend and this new guy. I was having so much fun with the new guy that I was avoiding the other one. I kept receiving phone calls from my ex-boyfriend who was trying to track me down, but I was ignoring him. He finally found me down at the bar. He was so mad when I told him about the new person that I had been seeing. He still tried to work it out between us, but I was past that point. He spent one more night with me until he didn't want to see me anymore. We got into a huge fight and it was finally over. Great sex or not. It was better that it happened this way because he had already broken my heart. I wasn't about to let him do it again. Although I missed him and did try to reach out to apologize for my behavior he never replied. By him not responding back made it easier for me to move forward.

I had enough nonsense with men breaking my heart. I decided that I was just going to have fun with men instead of being serious with them. I started to try crack-cocaine and was smoking marijuana way more than I ever did because this new guy that I was dating was into it. I was so worn out from using different drugs that my body was feeling it. Instead of cocaine I was doing crack here and there. I was also occasionally using LSD. I still went to work and paid my bills, but I was slowly disappearing. The girl I was living with had a child and the father of her child had just moved out when I moved in. We were partying like crazy at her house, she was acting a little crazier than I was by sleeping around with any guy she could. I got so mad at her for doing this because she had a baby and I didn't think it was right. We got into a fist fight over it and our friends had to break it up. Things were out of hand and not to mention my period never came that month. I thought oh no not again.

I was partying so much that I didn't even realize that I could be pregnant. I thought it was due to the drug use because that can happen. I took a pregnancy test just to be sure and it came up positive. This was the second time I had gotten pregnant. I knew in my heart that this time around no matter what I would never abort another baby. I had already made up my mind about it. When I confronted the baby's father who I was pregnant by he was in shock, but he was so happy we were having a baby. We didn't know how we were going to bring everything together, but we worked hard to make everything happen. I can't tell you how different it felt to have a positive reaction from the father of our baby about being pregnant this time, that it changed my perspective on everything.

I was finally very happy. The very next person who I was so excited to tell was my mother. We approached her in the bar where she had been working and presented her with a gift. When she opened the gift inside she took out a bracelet that read "Grand-mom". At first, she was dumbfounded but then she got it, she realized that she was the one that was going to be a grand-mom. We were all so excited. We then took the next steps and got an apartment and then we got engaged. The journey was difficult because we needed the help of our families and money to get started but the baby shower that my mom worked so hard at putting together brought in everything we needed. It was a beautiful baby shower and it was one of the happiest moments of my life.

It was time for our baby to come! I was in labor for over fourteen hours and when he finally arrived it was a miracle. At that point, my whole world changed, and real love finally entered my life. I can't express the joy and the feeling you get when this miracle happens before your very eyes. All the pain that is associated with having a baby quickly leaves you and pure love floods your soul. There aren't words to express the overwhelming experience of childbirth.

The hardest part after giving birth was getting my son circumcised. I loved this little creation so much and was already in a protective mommy mode. Trying to make the decision to circumcise him was so difficult. I was so upset I couldn't stand the thought of them hurting my son for even one second and I cried. Of course, having all your hormones turned upside down from pregnancy doesn't help the process. Before I knew it was all over with and he was sound asleep. We then took our beloved son home with us. Everyone came to visit him and love on him it was such a happy time. I wouldn't trade it for the world.

When my son Brandon entered my life everything that seemed important to me vanished and he was all that mattered. He became all that was good in the world. Having a child changes your life forever. Things are never the same again, in a good way! No longer does your life belong to you it belongs to your children. It is true there isn't a manual that comes with having a baby but somehow God made sure to put the instincts inside of us to learn quickly. My mother came to our home and stayed for a couple of weeks to help us out. Which was such a blessing.

After my son, Brandon came home with us and I had some time to experience motherhood, I realized that I didn't have the same desires to smoke and drink like I used to. I didn't have to drink all day or everyday like before I got pregnant. I was completely sober and drug free during my pregnancy. I didn't smoke either. I started to drink again after he was born. I would only get drunk after I put my son to bed. One night I got so terribly drunk that I had to wake my son's father up and have him call out of work, so he could take care of our son. It was then that I knew something had to change! I realized that my previous lifestyle no longer suited me.

I not only wanted to stop drinking I was feeling the urges to quit smoking, drinking and drugs altogether. Childbirth and being a mother changed me. Making different decisions changed my life. If you are driven to be self-sufficient for most of your life, then I suggest you wait to have children because they will change everything and the same things that you used to do will not be a part of your normal daily routine anymore. It sounds great in theory when your little and you make up this perfect family in your head. But how many of you reading this know it doesn't work that way for most us. I used to say when I was growing up that I wanted to be married with two children, one boy and one girl and everything will be perfect. Nothing was even close to that.

Soon my relationship with my fiancé was getting estranged. I felt like I wanted to change but I didn't see him react with those same feelings. I was growing up as a new parent and he wasn't. I was staying home with our son every day and he was still going about his normal routine and hanging out with his friends.

This was the beginning of severing our relationship. I was understanding that life held a lot more responsibilities that I was not prepared for, but I didn't have a choice I had to take care of my son. You see when your pregnant although things are changing inside your body, the responsibilities haven't quite changed yet because you still have your freedom but once the baby comes into the world there are two of you instead of one now.

Although a father is in the home it doesn't mean that he is tending to the needs of the family. When the outside world is still more important than the immediate family something is wrong. This is what caused us to argue quite often. The once fun going crazy lifestyle between the two of us had ended at least for me. At this point in my life I was already starting to lose the urge to smoke weed, drink, and smoke cigarettes. I had stopped doing hard drugs and had cut back on my drinking. I was welcoming this change that was tugging on my heart. He wasn't ready for anything to change which caused a division between us.

While we were still together my sons father and I had a mutual friend, he liked to come over and visit us at our apartment. He loved to smoke marijuana. When he would visit us the first thing he would do is pull up a chair and pull out his paraphernalia and roll a joint. I always made sure my son was sleeping or he wasn't allowed to smoke in our apartment. Then the funniest thing would happen, he would start talking to us about God as he puffed on his weed. Well of course my fiancée wasn't interested in anything but smoking his friends pot but for some reason I would sit there and listen to him. When this friend would come over, he would talk to me about Jesus and how there was a Heaven and a Hell. He would leave me literature so that in my private time I could better understand who God was.

I was confused at first, I had no idea what this new concept about God was. I mean I had always believed there was a God or at least someone more powerful than me who answered my prayers in a time of desperation. Remember I shared with you in some chapters back about some visions that I had or prayers that I would pray to stay out of trouble? These things helped prepare me for the gospel that I was getting ready to receive into my life.

The closest I ever came to being a religious person was by having a bible on my bureau in my bedroom that my step-father gave me. The only thing I used it for was to hide my valuables in it, like I thought everyone else did. After all isn't that what we use the bible for? No one ever taught me that I could read it. I did try to read the information that our friend gave me, but I just couldn't understand it. It intrigued me and when he would visit I asked every question I could think of to get some answers.

I was trying to challenge my friend, but I could not escape the thoughts of this God whom he was speaking about. It seemed more interesting than ever to get to know God. Now some religious groups would say how can a guy who is in sin smoking weed witness to you about God? My answer is simple? I don't know but it's true. That is exactly how I came to invite God into my life. I believe that when your searching for something way beyond your own reasoning God has no problem stepping in like a gentleman to walk you through the process of getting to know Him. In whatever ways, He sees fit to do so. It's the way He captures your attention.

As I pondered this God, I would lay awake and question in my mind was He all that this man has said He is? I laid there and thought about how as a little girl and as an adult he visited me and then it came to me very quickly that this Jesus, this God has been pursuing me all my life and I had never acknowledged Him until now!

Our friend came over again one night and said if you want to know God for yourself just pray to Him and He will answer you. He then invited us to go to church with him to celebrate Thanksgiving and to have dinner at the church and meet some new people. So, we all decided that we would go to church together as a family and see what it was all about. I listened to the sermon and then afterwards I had the pleasure of meeting the Pastor. I had so many questions for him. I was trying to challenge this notion of the God they were talking to me about to see if this God withstood the test of time, because if you know me I am a very determined person and I want answers.

I remember the Pastor being patient with me beings I was new to all of this. So, to help me out with my doubt he gave me an example. He said if I lay these keys on the pew and your son (who was only age one at the time) came and took these keys, he said would that be stealing? I answered I guess but he is just a baby. But he replied, "it doesn't change the act of what he did therefore he is sinning against God." Well, that struck a nerve in me, I thought no way! What my baby a sinner, never!

Then God made sure that the truth the Pastor spoke to me that night sunk into my heart. When the act is revealed in your heart you are responsible for the choices you have made whether you are conscious of it or not. "There needed to be someone named Jesus who would take our place so that way we would be able to enter into His Heaven when we die", said the Pastor. That whole night my perspective on everything he said had shifted me into a whole new world.

My relationship was now being challenged with my fiancée because he wasn't interested in God. He didn't want to go to church with me anymore. Despite how my fiancée felt I was ready to meet God one way or another. So, one night when everyone was asleep in bed and I was all alone I knelt beside my sofa and I asked God to prove to me that he was real and that He existed. I prayed a prayer like this: Lord if your real show me, please deliver me from this hell that I am in and rescue me. Come into my heart now and please forgive me of my past!

Immediately at that moment at the end of my prayer as I said my last word I felt a pin prick touch my heart as if someone had opened the door and walked right on in. I suddenly felt these weights that were very heavy feeling lift off my shoulders as if I was a prisoner being set free and I felt forgiven from all my past burdens and mistakes! I knew that night my life had changed. I could not stop talking about what happened to me and how Jesus came into my life and all by a simple honest prayer to want to know HIM!

Three days later after I prayed this prayer I no longer smoked, drank, or touched another street drug in my life. That is how powerful God is. He can change your situation in an instant. I started attending church regularly and I became a part of the family of God. My fiancée on the other hand was so angry that we were not having sex anymore and that I was clean and sober for the first time in my life that he decided to move out. While I was growing in God his lifestyle was getting worse.

While being separated, we tried to make it work for my son's sake, but it just wasn't the same. We were now two completely different people. He was unhappy that this property(me) was no longer available to him. I knew at that point that this relationship had to end permanently, and it did. We hardly ever saw him again until years later.

I started to have a prayer life with God. I would ask Him to show me how to straighten the mess out that was going on in my life. I became a single parent overnight. I didn't have enough income to get an apartment or to move into a new place. All I had at this point was Him. I slowly watched God sort out the details of my life one by one. I was hired as a waitress and I made good money. I was able to end my lease at the old apartment and I had saved up enough money to move into the new apartment that happened to be right below my mother and step-father's apartment. They watched my son while I worked, and God made sure that every need was met. It was amazing how I watched God's love at work in my life, seeing that He was real and that He was allowing the things that would try to harm me to be thwarted and turned to good for me and my son's sake. He answered my prayers to let me know He was real and did exist!

I continued to grow strong in God. I attended the church that my past friend had introduced me to. I became a part of their family. I learned how to use my faith and to believe God for the impossible things. Things that I knew I could never accomplish on my own. I saw the blessings all around me. I could work three or four days a week and be home with my son for the rest of the week. I made enough money to have a shorter work schedule. My apartment was right below my mother's and I don't know how God orchestrated that, but it was perfect for us. God was knitting our family together because He knew I needed her support more than ever if I was going to succeed as a single parent. What is the probability that I could live right under my mother in an apartment complex at that exact time that I needed to be? Miracles were truly happening for me.

Lesson Learned: I thought I was a truly independent person who didn't need anyone. Apparently, that couldn't be further from the truth because I kept seeking out these hideous relationships. Could it be that I was attracting someone with the same broken tendencies that I had and just didn't notice? I don't think I realized how truly broken I was in the first place which made me vulnerable to people who were just as messed up as I was. I was like this big magnet pulling in people who I could help because they had issues, yet I couldn't even resolve my own problems. They say like attracts like. They also say opposites attract too. I believe like attracts like is referring to people who are both mentally stable or both broken. They attract after their own kind. So, if two people are level headed they both can figure out the problem and move forward. If the two people are broken, then they are fractured in their hearts and they'll constantly hurt each other and create more issues. The matter of opposites attracting to opposites is questionable too. Sometimes people want what they can't have because the opposite of themselves looks interesting. When they wind up getting what they want and find out that the person with an opposite personality irritates them then their miserable because they have nothing in common with the person who is their opposite. So, what is the solution here? Where is the happy medium? Let's look at reality. Relationships in themselves are difficult because there are two people trying to merge their lives into one. How can that successfully happen when the two people in a relationship don't even know what they want or need. In my broken place, I couldn't understand why I kept getting involved with men that would break my heart repeatedly. Why didn't some of these men want to marry me? I'll tell you why. The answer was never going to be found in the men I was with because they were just the in between fix. It's like a junkie who does the same repetitious thing over and over with drugs but never achieves anything different from their situation. The real answer lied within myself all along. I could never help anyone to get better or fix themselves when I still needed fixing. Sometimes we become the mirror image of the very thing that we are trying so desperately to escape from. We don't always see hope because we've darkened our own hearts from allowing real love to come in. I was looking for the right man, but I wasn't the right woman yet. How could I be in a relationship that functioned normally when I wasn't prepared for it myself. Sometimes we need to get out of our own way. It takes courage! So, if your standing in your own way please move out of your way. Fight for yourself and give yourself the opportunity to see where the true problem lies and fix it. Do it in whatever ways you can so that the burdens become lighter and your days get happier. Let yourself be free from the burdens that cause depression and anxiety. Let yourself be You! Let's start here. Take a piece of paper out or a little note pad and carry it with you. Then take notice when you do something that upsets you about yourself and it seems to frustrate you. Then write it down on paper. Don't dwell on it. No pity parties allowed. Do this for one week and at the end of the week see how many times you've annoyed yourself in that certain area. Then you're going to find the solution to that problem. When you get the solution, don't give up. Give yourself a chance to work on it. It may take some time. Remember you didn't get there overnight so it won't be gone overnight. Give yourself a break. It's a process. The key is to stick with your solution so that you make the progress that your looking to achieve. You must build your relationship with yourself first. Now go get started!

John 3:16- For God so loved the world that He gave His only begotten Son, that whoever believes in Him should not perish but have everlasting life.

Chapter 7- I Got Married!

     I was attending church faithfully. I was enjoying this new transformation that was taking place in my life. I was finally becoming a clear minded person who was sober and focused on being an excellent mom. I was working and maintaining my own income while being completely single. I had a great set of friends who became my family at the church where I was attending. We were always doing something together whether it was inside or outside of the church. We would go door to door to introduce people to our church and invite them to the service. On occasion, we would have a few visitors come but not too many. About one year later a new visitor had arrived at our church. He was a male in his late forties. He had recently accepted God into his life. He was the friend of a couple who had already been attending our church. He was so full of life and very happy to be in the family of God that He would talk about nothing else except how God had changed his life. Everyone in the church loved it when we got new visitors because it brought a new zeal into the church.

     We were a very close knit but small congregation. We held a lot of pot luck dinners. We had a choir. We didn't have many children attending at the time except for my son so we were all mainly adults. The new man that came to our church started attending regularly and joined the choir. He also started to attend our church dinners and eventually became a member of the church. He became very close with the Pastor. I was already close to my Pastor as well as he considered me to be like his daughter beings he and his wife had only sons.

     This new member had no problem introducing himself to people. He was a very outspoken person. One day while at church he happened to come over to where a friend and I was having a conversation and politely interrupted it. He was talking to us about how he needed to get a bed for his new apartment. How ironic, I just happened to be getting rid of one. He made a promiscuous joke about the bed in passing which was rather odd beings we were in the church surrounded by others. It was like a subliminal pass being sent to me. I just ignored it.

Taking care of my son was the only thing on my mind at this point. As he and I both continued to attend the same church we quickly became aware of the fact that we were drawn to each other. I soon found out that he had six children. I had never been married before nor had I been with a man that had other children, so it was all new to me. I welcomed the fact that he had children because I had a son too. He was much older than I was, but I didn't worry about that because I had always hung out with older people all my life. I was more impressed by his maturity and charm. He did have a certain magnetism about himself. I also loved the fact that his children and my older son had developed a relationship and they all got along so well. I started to realize that maybe we had more in common than I thought.

I had been completely celibate purposefully up to this point and I honored that fact about myself. By having a relationship with God, it helped me to bring honor to my body instead of shame. Like I had in the past. I had gone on only two dates prior to meeting this new male church member. On one of those dates it started heading in the wrong direction, so I ended that very quickly and the second date that I went on, the guy was still seeing another woman. So, neither of those dates panned out for me.

Our church had a get together on Christmas Eve. We were having a little celebration with refreshments following the service. We were all in attendance including our newest member and having a good time fellowshipping with one another. It was coming time to leave the celebration and as I was heading out the door, this man (the newest member) had no ride home, so he asked me if I wouldn't mind giving him a ride. So, I said yes. I was not sure what was happening here by me saying yes but beings people at our church always helped each other out I didn't think anything of it. I especially didn't want to be rude at Christmas time.

When we arrived at his apartment complex I had asked if I could use his phone because I was running behind schedule to pick my son up. We didn't have cell phones at the time. He said sure. I made my phone call and told my mother that I was on my way. I then got ready to leave when he said would you like a cup of tea? I said sure. We sat and talked for a bit. Then he also made us a tuna-fish sandwich to eat with our tea. When we had finished eating and drinking our tea I told him I needed to be leaving. As I was heading towards the door he thanked me for the ride and kissed me on the cheek as he said goodbye. We exchanged phone numbers that night.

We all arrived at church for service on Christmas Day and my newest male friend had brought my son a Christmas gift and gave it to him. I thought how kind is that for him to think of my son. Not long after that we started dating. Our Pastor was not happy about us dating. He didn't like the fact that he was many years older than I was and had many children from previous relationships. I didn't know all the details at the time we started to date except for what he had told me about his family. He said that he was separated and lived in his own apartment. He told me that his previous relationship had been over for a long time. What did I know? I believed him.

Before I dated him, I sought counsel from my Pastor, but I didn't reveal who the person was that I was going to date. When I was seeking advice from my Pastor at the time there was another man who was interested in me as well. There wasn't a disregard not to date anyone from my Pastor at the time of the counseling session, he just told me to see how it goes. So, I figured okay why not date this guy. After dating for a few weeks New Year's Eve had approached us, so I took him to a family party and I introduced him to my mother and her fiancée. My mother looked surprised because unbeknownst to me she had already knew this man. We stayed briefly and then I took him home. Later, she had told me that he was bad news. I had explained to her that he wasn't like that anymore and had changed.

My mother didn't care for this man because of his history with drugs and owing people lots of money. She knew what type of reputation he had before I ever met him. I believed that was his past and because I had changed I thought that he had changed too. By appearances it sure seemed like he had. Could he finally be the one? I loved his kids and the way he so easily loved my son that it all seemed too good to be true.

What attracted me to him was that he had a certain *je-ne-sais-quoi* about himself. It was very attractive at first until I got to know him. I found out a lot more about him as time went on like how he came from a dysfunctional family and that he was dysfunctional himself when it came to a family life. I didn't know that until we were already too involved. We had already grown to liking each other a lot and because I wasn't fully healed from being broken in my past relationships I was compassionate towards him regarding these things. I found out that some of his past baggage was that he used to be a hustler. All this was before his conversion. He seemed like a new person, so I didn't pay much attention to it.

When our Pastor found out that we were seriously dating each other he was totally against it and had no problem telling me so. At the time, my Pastor gave me this advice our church was splitting up and I didn't value his input anymore. There was something that happened between the Pastor and the new man in my life, but I never knew what it was. Whatever happened it was enough to make my new man leery about church folks. This is where my new man changed once again. He didn't seem to have that overwhelming passion for God like he did when he first came to the church.

As we were getting serious and hanging out with each other all the time I started to see the dysfunctional side of his behavior come out more and then I understood why our previous Pastor had been against the relationship. I started noticing things like him lying about where he had been or who he was with. He would say one thing and then do another. His stories never matched up with what he was saying and doing. Now I may have been naïve, but I was not stupid. He would tell me that he wasn't doing drugs but when I confronted him with proof he quickly came up with a story to cover his lies.

Another strange incident was that he was still in an active ongoing relationship with his ex who lived only minutes away from both our homes. He could walk into her home at any time without even knocking on the door, that seemed odd to me because most exes are not that close. His ex would give him rides because he didn't have a car. I found that out when I saw them passing me by on the road one day. At this point I honestly did try to break off the relationship. I was changing myself. I was trying to work on me. I didn't need more drama in my life. So, I told him that I didn't think that our relationship was going to work out. Immediately after I broke up with him he showed up at my door with flowers, in tears and was apologizing to me profusely saying that it would never happen again. He would write me love poems and call me his special lady. You know things that would melt your heart, how could I not forgive him?

Then I caught him smoking cigarettes. He said he had quit smoking. It never seemed to end. So of course, I gave him one more chance. I believed that he was trying to come out of an old lifestyle and start a new one and I knew that it would take some time to adjust. I tried to have patience with him, but my fuse was getting low. To top all of that off I had been celibate for over a year prior to meeting him. No sex. Can you believe it? Me, not having sex. It was a miracle. As Christians, we don't believe in having sex before marriage. We save ourselves for that special someone. Me being celibate for that long meant a lot especially because in the past I use to do the opposite and give myself away. So, I worked hard at not being the old me.

Honestly when I met him sex was not on my mind, marriage was. But the longer we were dating and the more we were together it tempted us. Some many months later he and I gave into the temptations by not following boundaries and staying accountable to someone else. We wound up eventually having sex and we were not married. It became difficult for us to be together without having sex. After wards I would cry because I would feel so guilty. I knew that what I was doing was not pleasing to God. How could I do that to Him after all He has done for me I thought. It was a hard situation to be in. I was condemning myself over it.

It started out very innocently. He just came over for dinner and then before we knew it we wound up on the couch and then we started kissing and then one thing lead to another. It happened so quickly. It was like trying out a new drug for the first time. It was exciting and sad all at the same time. The first time is always the hardest to get through but the more you keep doing it you get addicted to it. I still felt ashamed after we would have sex. I was saving myself for when I got married. I cried because I felt like I had failed. We both told God that we would never let it happen again. Guess what? Words are cheap, boundaries were still not in place and we did it several more times. I finally couldn't take it anymore and I told him how cheap I felt and that he would have to make an honest woman out of me because I felt like a prostitute in God's eyes.

It was eating away at my heart and mind so bad that I had to speak with him honestly about the problem. I told him that what we were doing was wrong and that if this relationship was going to continue then he would have to marry me. I told him that he would have to make an honest woman out of me before God. I didn't realize what I was saying! It was already a bad relationship with all the lying and not knowing where he was half the time and now we were having sex. I felt helpless and out of control. Now I was deciding out of guilt and shame instead of getting counsel for the situation. Our church had just split, and we weren't connected to another church yet, so I didn't know where to turn for help. So, I made my own decision out of fear.

Looking back in hindsight I could have just repented to God and asked for His forgiveness and for Him to have mercy on me so that I could move forward and break off the relationship. He would have easily forgiven me, but I was never taught that part of Christianity. I learned how I should react to situations by legalism and rules in the church and not by the grace of God on my life.

This is where you need to hear me. We hung out too much alone! This is a big No-No. It only takes one time being alone for it to happen. If there are no boundaries there is bound to be trouble brewing. I was a Christian woman longer than he was a Christian man and I knew better than to fall into some of the traps that were being set for me. I was so vulnerable at the same time because my heart wanted the whole marriage dream, with the white picket fence and the happily ever after. I just wasn't willing to wait for the right one. I had desires that I thought were being fulfilled by God, but it was my own flesh that was orchestrating the whole thing.

I saw all the signs around me that something wasn't right. I saw that our previous Pastor was against our relationship for a reason. I knew it when I tried to find a local church to marry us and I couldn't find one clergy person who would. I even tried finding someone in another state and couldn't find anyone that would marry us. No one was calling me back. That right there should have been a giant red flag notifying me that the answer was NO. Do not marry this man!

I did just the opposite anyhow. I wound up marrying him on a whim. We drove all the way down to another state to the justice of the peace. It was not on a day that we picked out for a special occasion, like our wedding day. It was a last-minute thing. We went before I had to go to work that day. We took my son Brandon with us to be our witness and we got married. There were no other family members, no church building, and no reception afterwards. When it was all over I changed into my work clothes and drove to work.

He didn't even buy me a wedding ring. I had used my engagement ring from my son's father and bought a bridge for it with my income tax return. I did that on my own because he didn't have the money to get a ring when we got married. I bought into the lie that he told me when we were first dating, which was, I may not have a lot of money, but I will always love you and never cheat on you and I believed him.

This whole decision to get married happened because I came out of a church that was on the harder side of religion. Instead of having that intimate relationship with God that allows U-turns, I thought that God was mad at me. So, I was going to fix this mess myself for God. I wanted to please Him. So, in my own human efforts I tried to fix what I did wrong. I totally missed the whole concept of "Grace" in my life. That is always our problem as humans. God provides the grace when we mess up and don't know any better, but we think were condemned because we failed Him. This is a lie that is taught by some religions, yet it is not the truth. God can take care of Himself. We don't need to fix anything for Him. Now I am not saying that we can keep continuing to stay in sin and make the same mistakes over and over. That is not at all what I mean. But "Grace" is there for you to learn from your mistakes. His grace gives us the freedom to learn how to do things differently, so we never do those things again because we found a better way. Then we can share that better way with others. We can teach them how to avoid the same mistakes we made through our experiences and forgiveness.

Lesson Learned: Stick to your convictions! And, please pay attention to the signs around you. They are there to direct you. Stay with your gut instincts. Nine times out of ten they are there to warn you. It's the human nature in us that causes us to shut our eyes to the truth. We would rather have a little pleasure for a while, which we know is wrong and thus we then have a lifetime of struggles because of it. This leaves us wondering what happened to our lives? One thing I learned from this is never, never buy your own engagement ring! That itself shows that you have no value or worth to the other person. If a man can't buy a woman a ring, any kind of ring, he isn't worthy of your love. That ring that he purchases for you isn't just bling-bling, it is a symbol of eternal love. A covenant made between two people of whom God has joined together and who vows to remain as one while on the Earth. It's not just a piece of paper. Also, don't trust anyone who gives you one excuse after another. Break-free! That's bondage. Oftentimes we are so hard on ourselves that we can't even give ourselves some of the things that we deserve. We miss great opportunities because of it. When we do this, we fall victim to what's of lesser value for our lives. Now, if your already in a relationship like this, then you need to get some help. It's not healthy. If you truly love that person or yourself then that is what you can do for each other, get healthy together. When two people are operating out of a different mindset that is contrary to bringing agreement in the relationship then it won't work. When one is lying, or sleeping around the relationship will never work. We must have pure motives and pure hearts towards one another. God will not allow one person to take advantage of the other person. You'll know this is happening because there will be constant friction between the two of you. If you try to get help and it still doesn't work which is what happened in my situation, then don't feel guilty if that person isn't willing to change. Move on knowing that you tried everything possible to make it work and leave the rest up to God. Unity is the key in every relationship. It's all God asks for. It is the glue that holds people together especially during trying times. Please, don't go run off and get married! Your wedding day is a special day. Whether it is elaborate or a very simple wedding, your loved ones should be there to celebrate this special occasion with you. I learned never will I run off, get married, not include my family, and go to work after. Let this be a lesson to all of you reading this. Many things can cause someone to get married, but guilt should never be a reason that you do. Beloveds, please remember that if we make these mistakes let's not beat ourselves over the head. Always remember that God's grace supersedes any mistakes that we could ever get into. It overrides guilt. Guilt makes you feel like you need to make everything perfect or right in man's eyes. Grace allows you to forgive yourself. So, allow grace to have its perfect work in your life and learn from it. No one should have to go through a lifetime of mental or emotional abuse from another person, this is a definite red flag! Love is to be shared between two people who desire the best for one another. Who stick together in the good times as well as the bad times. Love is sensual when shared between two soul mates. There should never be envy, jealousy, pride, or negative criticism that controls or hurts the other person's soul. Lastly, I must mention that God does not like divorce. His word is clear on that, but He also does not stand for abuse either. Remember not everyone is who they appear to be. It does take some time to get to know someone. Even if you find yourself with butterflies in your stomach or thinking of that person every minute of the day and your clicking so well, give it some time. People always change after the honeymoon is over so to speak. So, get to know one another's thoughts, patterns, and habits. God gave us time for a reason. I believe this is one of them. Time will tell is what they say. Time also heals wounds. Both are true. I'd rather put into practice the phrase time will tell then time will heal my wounds. We can avoid the latter if we take our time. Evaluate any relationships that feel damaging to your soul and look for the signs, God will guide you to all truth. Then you will have the knowledge to know better when it is trying to happen again, and you can run! Be liberated~

Proverbs 4:23 – Guard your heart above all else, for it determines the course of your life.

In the beginning, whatever this guy told me I believed him. He appeared to be a good dad and I know he loves his kids. But I wasn't prepared for the baggage that he was bringing with him into our relationship. I was so naïve to that kind of stuff. He was older than me and seemed to have been around the block more than I have been, so I trusted him. He worked for himself and he made it seem like he made a good living at what he did and that he was just hitting rough patches with his work being slow at times. So once again I believed him. Remember I always said he had charisma. He could easily talk himself out of anything.

So now we are married, and it was nothing but a rollercoaster ride from day one. First, you can't love someone fully unless you are healed and love yourself first. This was our problem. I recognized the need for change in my life and I didn't want to continue to suffer anymore but he did the opposite he kept years of pain and hurt lying beneath his wounds which made our relationship trouble. Yes, he claimed to be a Christian, but he was not doing what it took for himself to get healing and move forward. No matter how much we went to church and participated in functions together or had bible studies in our home he just slowly slipped further and further away from God. He was living a double life. When you don't take care of your past and your present isn't in order nothing changes. Regardless of the struggle and the many nights I cried myself to sleep my beliefs were once you were married that you were to stay married unless there was infidelity. That was what I was taught. So, I decided to stay married to him.

After about a year of being married we found out that we were pregnant with our first child together. It was a boy. The marriage was still bad, but this was good news and it brought some hope to our family. It was a very difficult pregnancy and I was hospitalized a couple of times because I was so sick and couldn't eat. When I was about six months pregnant the morning sickness wore off and I could start eating properly which helped me feel better.

My son arrived two weeks late. I had to have an unplanned C-section with him. But when he came into our lives it was such a blessing! He was a big baby when he was born. What a joy he brought to our family. Now I had two sons whom I loved with all my heart. Things were a little better with my son's father at the time, but he still believed that all he had to do was bring home money and that was his only job. My husband was still the same person he always was, and he didn't go out of his way to do anything differently after our son arrived. We still argued a lot. It was the same story all over again with my second baby's father who was just like the first baby's father. They did not want to give up their own lifestyle for anyone.

I was raising two kids and his kids on the weekends and I eventually went back to work because we couldn't afford for me to be a stay at home mom. I had credit cards that were maxed out because of the lack of income. I would have to use the credit cards to buy food, pay his child support, pay the bills, and buy things for our kids. There was no intimacy in our relationship. I would recall times that I wanted to be with my husband when we were all alone and he would refuse. I should have seen the signs then. Prior to that I found out that he was using drugs again here and there. So, when that was happening either him or I would leave our home to stay somewhere else.

Meanwhile he had a way of wriggling himself back into our home after he left. I can't count how many times I kicked him out or I moved out and we got back together. I can tell you we had more than five counselors who tried to help us put the marriage back together but when one person isn't willing to change it won't work. I had enough of the police coming to our home and our neighbors knowing all our business. I got tired of appearing like things were okay. Yet everything was nothing but lies. He looked great on the outside but inside he was a whole different person. I till this day can't say that I knew him like I thought I did. Isn't it amazing that you can live with someone for several years and still not know them?

As a hurting woman, I needed help. I had to take medication to keep myself calm. One night we got into a terrible fight and I was at my wits end. I was so worn out that I had taken about five nerve pills over time to get rid of the pain and frustration that was tormenting me. I took them about thirty minutes apart. I wasn't trying to overdose or commit suicide. I just wanted relief from the anxiety of it all. I never took that many pills before. I decided to go into the shower to get some peace and privacy and I cried and prayed for relief. Instantly God sobered me up supernaturally. I was completely sober! He saw the danger that I was bringing upon myself and He saw the demons in my life that were trying to destroy me. He saw the breakdown that I was having, and He intervened. It was a miracle that I was instantly sober. At that moment, I realized that true love comes from God and that He does care for me. He was there when my husband wasn't. In the shower, I heard the audible voice of God say "NO" and I walked out of the shower as if I had not touched one pill. Who knows if I would have overdosed or slipped in the shower and hit my head, anything could have happened, but God said "NO". This is another encounter I had of God's protection and love.

I stayed in the marriage regardless of the struggles because I made a vow before God and as Christians we don't get divorced unless it's for infidelity. It wasn't pleasant being in an abusive relationship. I was dead inside. Numb. I hardly laughed or smiled during the whole seven years we were married. Yet I wanted to remain faithful to my commitment to God because He had been so good to me. Even if I did it out of guilt, God understood my heart. I am a woman of my word and just because my marriage was failing me doesn't mean that God would.

The relationship continued although we had nothing in common and were just two opposites existing under the same roof. We parented differently, we wanted to handle our finances differently and we never agreed on anything. Out in public we would put on our happy faces and pretend like everything was great, but it wasn't. I hated the life I was living.

Our home now became as dysfunctional as we were. It was tough on our kids when they constantly saw us fighting. My fear was always that my boys were going to think that this is how a marriage is supposed to work and it's not!

The abuse emotionally and physically was escalating. I eventually got a restraining order on him because he wouldn't leave the house. It was the only way to get him out of my life for the moment, so I could breathe. He finally moved out once again and I found some peace.

Lesson Learned: God is my source! His is my protector and my provider. He guides me along the paths of wisdom and keeps me sane! He shows up when no one else does. The journey is real and so is the struggle. Sometimes in life we will go through things alone. We hide from others and pretend that everything is okay when we know that things couldn't be farther from the truth. I've learned that there is at least one person in my circle that I can turn to for help and that's God. I never want to see any one of you drowning in the sea of life. Please reach out for help if you need it. To God or your best friend. To those who you can trust and feel safe with. There is no shame or guilt in trying to rise above abuse in any form. You must get out of any abusive relationship. Whether it is emotional or physical abuse or both. The more you stay involved in this type of relationship the more brain washed you become. The more beaten down you will be. This will lead you to feel like a victim for the rest of your life. You're not doing anyone any favors by staying in a victim mode especially not for yourself or your loved ones. They need you! There is a place where you can fall into a victim mentality, but you don't have to stay there. You must become victorious! This world needs hero's like you. We need conquerors who are not wounded anymore on the battle field and who are raging against the tides to rise above defeat. You weren't given this beautiful life to be defeated by others who don't want you to have a better life. There is no failure in wanting to transform all the dead things going on inside of you or externally outside of you. This is our life and we are the captains of it and we steer the ship. We get to navigate where were heading to. No one gets to take that away from us! Seek out counsel and get some help. Improve your life. It's up to you to do it. People will rarely ask you if you need help. They have enough problems of their own. That's why you're going to have to find the strength from within to get help. You must take the necessary steps to get where you want to be. One day at a time.

Everyone's journey is different, so you can't compare your situation to the next persons. But, you can find people who are going through similar problems. Find people who will help you get your vision back. Your entitled to this life! You are not someone's slave, babysitter, housekeeper, sex object or sugar momma. God wonderfully and fearfully made you. He has a plan for your life you just need to seek Him to find out the directions on how to get there. Pray, meditate. Find the answers because they are out there. Have hope. It's such a powerful tool to have. It gives you wings to expect the unexpected! It allows things to happen to you in positive ways. It gives you butterflies in your belly. It leaves you anxious with good thoughts. All the things that make you move forward are wrapped up in faith, hope, and love. Don't pretend everything is all right when it isn't. Make it right with in your soul. Keep yourself aligned. Then everything will come together, and it will be better than before. People are counting on you and me to be there in a time of crisis. But how can we do that unless we help ourselves first, right? You have so much to offer this world don't ever sell yourself short. I want to suggest that you speak one positive thing a day over yourself or any situation that you want to see change. Plan a strategy. Get a vision board and put all the things you plan to accomplish on it. Use pictures and phrases. Whatever it is that you want on the board put it on there. You can put a time limit on your goals or not. The point is that you have something in front of your eyes to look at every day to encourage you to keep on moving forward. Do that for a few weeks and I bet your outlook on life will be brighter. Your vision of how you see yourself and your future will start to enlarge. Be mindful of yourself. Your opinions matter!

Proverbs 4:7 – Getting wisdom is the wisest thing you can do! And whatever else you do, develop good judgement.

Chapter 9- The Death of My Son Brandon

My oldest son was seven and so bright. He was beautiful in looks and extremely intelligent. He could read the newspaper at age five. I remember how this fascinated us. He was crowned little Mr. Gloucester of our city and was in love with baseball. He was so happy when his little brother came into the picture and he fell in love with him instantly. They were inseparable. My younger son literally hung around his big brother's neck that is how much he loved him so. They had their little tit for tats over toys but that's about it. I was a single parent with my first son for a few years until I met my first spouse. We all gelled together like glue. My older sons step-father loved him just like he was his very own until the day he graduated to Heaven. My older son only knew him as his dad.

This part of my journey is so hard for me to share because no matter how many years have passed the situation is still real, even though I am healed. The absence of my son's presence will always be a place that no one can fill. Except God. I share this as part of my story for all of you who may have lost a child and can't seem to regain your strength. Please let yourself. Time does help the healing process. But you must give yourself a break before you give into grief forever. The absence of a loved one who has gone on will always be there but your love for them is what will carry you through.

I will never forget this day. I was getting ready for work like every other ordinary day and anyone who knows me knows that I tend to run late. I have gotten better but I still have not fully arrived. This was one of those days. I was hurrying my older son Brandon and telling him that we needed to go and that he should have had his things packed by now to sleep over Nanny and Pops house. It was a frustrating conversation between me and my older son only because I was stressed. I never knew when or if my estranged husband would show up or not to watch the kids.

On this day, he was not there to watch them before I left, and I was running behind schedule. I proceeded to help my son Brandon get his overnight bag ready and I got both kids into the car. As I was driving to my mother's apartment I suddenly felt a compulsion to apologize to my older son. I listened to that prompting and I told him that I was sorry because I got a little heated with him about not being ready to go to Nanny and Pops house. I held his hand all the way to my mom's apartment and I told him I loved him when I dropped him off.

Prior to this day, we had a birthday party for both of my boys because their birthdays were one month apart from each other. Financially for us it was easier to do their birthdays together. This was the first year we ever decided to do it this way. Many things in life are no coincidence. Things seem to happen for a reason even though we don't realize it at the time.

Now, I had just dropped my kids off at my mother's and was on my way to work. My sons had run upstairs and forgot all about me because they were on their way to see Pops who loved them dearly. Later that day my older son went from my mom's apartment over to his cousin's house to sleep over and spend some time with them. It was summer break. At this point I was separated once again from my husband because that was always the case between us. My mother used to say that me and the kids lived with her and Pops more than we did with my own husband. She was right.

It was getting near the end of my shift at work. I was wrapping things up when I received a phone call that changed my life forever! In the background, I could hear this woman screaming but I couldn't understand her. She just kept repeating the words "I needed to get to my mother's apartment because there had been a fire and to come quickly." I slammed the phone down and I immediately told my supervisor that I had to leave. I was praying franticly because I had no idea what was going on or what to expect. I didn't know who this woman was that called me or why there was a fire happening at my mother's apartment.

Earlier on in the evening my mother had plans to take both of my sons down to her neighbor's apartment who is a lifelong family friend, to celebrate her birthday. My sons played with her grandkids all the time. Her grandson was my son Brandon's best friend. Her birthday happened to be on that night and people were coming over her apartment to celebrate with her and her family. It was common for us to go over each other's homes to spend time together.

Later that evening Pops called down to my mother's friend's apartment so that my older son could come back to their apartment and watch one of their favorite television shows together. Pops and my older son had their special shows that they would watch together when my sons visited. My younger son was too young to do stuff like that. He was only four and didn't want to sit still and watch wrestling or baseball, but my older son loved this one on one time with his Pops.

My mom walked my son back down to their apartment. She returned to her friends where my younger son had been taking a nap. My older son had just returned to my mom's earlier that day from my cousin's house and was dropped off there because I was working. They always babysat for me when my estranged husband couldn't.

It was said that about thirty minutes later the fire had started from when my son Brandon went back to the apartment. My older son was in the bedroom and Pops was in the living room, this is how they were found. Apparently, my older son was tired and may have went to sleep in my mother's room because my cousin told me that when my son slept over his house they had stayed up all night playing video games. Everything that I write here is by word of mouth and reports. I was not there at the scene until afterwards.

As I am driving to my mother's apartment I had been so overtaken with thoughts of who got hurt but never imagined that anyone had died. I remember pulling up in my car and the complex was completely blocked off. I had to fight my way through the parking lot and through the police officers to tell them that I am family to these people that the fire is happening to. They quickly guided me into the parking lot leading to my mother's apartment.

I recall seeing flashing lights from the police cars and a bunch of chaos was going on in the parking lot. I was quickly making my way around the corner when my mom's friends husband approached me and before I could turn the corner he tried to get me to calm down. I was asking if everyone was all right? I kept repeating myself until someone answered me. The scene looked like it was from out of a movie. I started naming names and rambling on about where my kids were and no answer. I asked about my mom and her fiancé again and he finally spoke to me and said that Pops had died. I asked where the others were, and he looked at me with a sad face and I screamed at the top of my lungs and franticly started looking for my children. He assured me my kids were okay. I ran into the violent scene to see for myself what was happening.

I was approached by an officer who was taking me around to the apartment. A police officer was escorting me everywhere I went. I remember seeing an ambulance and my mother was inside it, so I tried to see her, they had her on oxygen. We tried to talk but we were both so upset. She was freaking out too much, so the authorities made me get out of the ambulance.

I was questioning the police where are my children?!! No one would tell me anything except that my older son was in route to the hospital. Two police officers then escorted me up to an apartment across from my mother's apartment. This was where my younger son was. As I looked back to my mom's apartment and surveyed the scene all I saw was chaos and black smoke bellowing through a huge hole in the top of the roof and the windows were blown out.

I ran up into the apartment as fast as I could. There was my younger son in the living room and he was safe, playing video games. I hugged him so tight and kissed him. After I was reassured that he was safe I was then approached by another police officer who said that he would give me a ride to the hospital. I still had no idea what was going on with my older son. No one would say a word. I asked why can't I drive there myself? He said that it would be better if he took me. I hugged my younger son again and left to go see my older son in the hospital. My mother's friends watched Elijah for me.

The officer drove me to the hospital and there was nothing but complete silence. We both walked into one of the sections of the hospital where I was told to wait for the nurse. I was inside a little cubicle off the main waiting room. It was pure white with minimal seating. The police officer waited outside of the room for me. As I walked the floors pacing and waiting franticly for someone to take me to go see my son Brandon a nurse turned the corner and approached me. It felt like I was in a part being played out of a movie script. She started asking me some questions about my son and if he was allergic to anything and then she disappeared. Immediately following her was the doctor who came in and broke the news to me.

All I heard coming from her lips were "your son has died and there was nothing that we could do." I immediately went into shock mode and denial. My whole body felt like all the blood in me had just drained out. My brain froze. I went blank. I screamed on the top of my lungs NOOOOOOOOOOOOOO!!! My knees went weak.

I was all alone when I got the news of my son's death, so I told them that I needed to call people. The hospital asked questions as to who they can call for me and I gave them some names. I wanted to go home and get some other phone numbers and call my estranged husband. The police officer was hesitant to take me home, but I demanded that he allow it. He took me home and followed me around the house as if he thought I might harm myself. Then he waited patiently for me to change and call some people.

He saw a picture of my son and asked me if that was him and I said yes. I could see that he was tearing up as he told me he was sorry. I made my phone call to my estranged husband and it did not go well. After I explained what happened to Brandon I heard the phone drop on the other end. It went silent. I had no more words to speak. I was numb and felt dead inside. I was then taken back to the hospital by the officer and was met there by my Pastor and his wife. They tried to console me.

My family started coming to the hospital one by one. My estranged husband finally arrived yet I was still in disbelief. My mother had to be taken away immediately to a hospital room because she saw too much and was delirious. She was trying to get into the apartment to find my son but couldn't and she had suffered from some smoke inhalation. She was disoriented about everything and thought my son was coming home. She kept asking when are they releasing him? Immediately I was approached by the organ donor people who were hounding me to donate. I couldn't even think straight, and I had all these people talking to me at one time, but everything was blank. I had no answers. All I could think about was my son.

They finally let my estranged husband and I go in and see my son Brandon after they had changed him and washed him. I was in shock. I was touching him and hugging him and checking his body as a protector would. My motherly instincts were on high alert. The valve that they had put into his arm was dripping blood and I was freaking out because they let this happen. I called the nurse to please take care of it immediately and she apologized.

As a mother, I was thinking of what I could do next to fix this whole thing, like what is my next move. I was bent on fixing this. After all isn't that what a mother does? I prayed to God to please raise my son back to life as I hung on to his body, but nothing happened. I remained silent. There were no words to describe this pain. I could do nothing but pace back and forth. I became robotic.

Family members came to see him, and I was just in denial as my family members were crying over my son's dead body. The hospital allowed this to go on until everyone got to see him and then they told us we had to leave. I was escorted away from my son. We were lead back into that little white box called a waiting room. I didn't want to leave. It was where I felt close to my son because I knew his body was there.

I remember being in that little room in the hospital for hours surrounded by loved ones and feeling dead and all alone as if no one was around me. Nothing anyone could try to say to me made any sense. My Pastor at the time was trying to give me sound advice on organ donation so the guy would leave me alone. Finally, I had decided to donate what we could. I know my son, if he could have had a say so he would have helped anyone. This was his small way of doing so.

That was an incredibly difficult decision to make at the time of my grieving, but I am glad I did it. This earthly body does not bind us. The Earth is not our destination but the spirit going back to Heaven is. I had to remember that even as I was heartbroken. We looked at it as if he was still doing good by helping someone else even after he had left us. He was still paying it forward even after his death. A little part of him would remain on the Earth so that someone else could benefit from such a tragedy.

Eventually it was getting very late and we finally left the hospital and met back at my house. My mother kept thinking that I was mad at her. She thought I didn't want her in my home. I was not even thinking about anything like that at this point. Through all the hurt and pain the first thing that I could hear clearly was God's voice. He spoke this word to me, "Forgive." He said if you don't forgive you will not show my love. At this point it was only God that was going to bring me through this horrific time in my life. He was the only one that I could hear clearly. I had to trust that He knew what was best for me in my frailty. He also knew what good was going to come out of this terrible loss in my life. He had never let me down before and has always come to my aide and rescue, so I knew He would do it for certain this time too.

I was a total mess. I had a house full of people constantly coming in and out. I had no concept of time nor did I know what day it was. I had no feeling in my body nor did I perceive any mental concepts of daily living. I was a complete invalid. I sat on my kitchen floor weeping for days. Surrounded by darkness. Thank God for my family for helping to take care of my younger son because I could not even do that. I literally felt like I was lying deep in the grave myself, alive, yet unable to crawl out of it. Just looking up from the bottom from time to time and feeling tormented day and night and feeling like I was never going to come out alive.

One day while I was sitting on my kitchen floor nestled in the corner of the cabinet, I visually saw myself in a grave and I could not take the torture anymore. The pain in my mind and body was too much to bear. If I could have literally ripped out my heart and mind I would have done so. In this moment, it was then that I heard the Lord speak loudly to the enemy of my soul in an audible voice. I heard Him say "Devil I rebuke you, leave her alone!" At that moment, I knew that God was still with me and that He was continually watching over me and protecting me because I was too frail to protect myself. I had to many countless hours of lying wide awake because I couldn't fall asleep. My mind was on autopilot. There was no logical thinking coming from my brain. I couldn't make any decisions. This is when the Lord started to strengthen me.

I would lie in my older son's bed, so I could finally fall asleep. But when I would awaken from sleep it would be to the same nightmare day after day and it was to the reality that he was gone. My heart just could not take it. I never wanted to fall asleep because I knew I would wake up to the devastating reality that he was no longer with us. I didn't know how to live a day without him. I had to take medicine to keep calm, stop crying and try to go to sleep. That didn't even help much.

When I couldn't sleep, I would drive to a twenty-four-hour Walmart and stay there until five or six in the morning, so I could wear myself out. I didn't eat for weeks at a time. I was rapidly losing a lot of weight. I had to seek counseling to be able to try and talk through his death. Even while taking all these steps it was not helping me. Do you know the only thing that kept me together was God! Nothing any human could say to me even in their genuine concern for my loss helped me. God's Spirit within me was the only thing keeping me afloat and strengthening me in my weakness.

I could not fully participate in the funeral process. The only thing I did was pick his outfit and flowers out with the help of family members. I don't know who did what. I was shown things, but my mind was void of all rationality. I didn't want to except any of it. I couldn't even look at pictures of my son or I would cry more. One thing I did go and do was to see my son before the day of the funeral. Being in this state of mind does not change the fact the you are still their mother and will act like one.

This sounds strange because of the situation but even in my grief I was so glad to see him if even in the casket. I made sure to look him over and I thought that he looked like he had too much blush on, so I alerted the funeral director and asked him to lighten up on the makeup and he did. I still wanted to take care of my son even though he was no longer a part of this earth. I still wanted to be his Mommy. Although he couldn't talk back to me it seemed comforting that he was in my presence. I had something tangible to hold onto and look at. I touched his cold, hard face with my lips and gave him a kiss goodbye and told him I loved him and that I would see him again tomorrow. This seemed to console me. Grief is nonsensical.

Tomorrow came and I was so disorderly. I didn't know what I was going to wear because I had lost so much weight. I just picked out the best thing I could find. So many people showed up at the viewing that there weren't enough seats for people to sit in. There was policeman, firefighters, school officials, etc. There was one officer who donated his badge and although he wasn't supposed to, he asked if I would do that for him in a beautiful letter that he had written to my family and I agreed.

While standing beside my son in the casket I was okay with greeting people like we were at a party. It was in honor of my son, so it was keeping me abroad. The service was heartfelt although I was a complete basket case. The only thing I remember was a song being sung called Eagles Wings. When the service was complete, and it was time to close the casket, I lost it. The separation was too much for me. I almost passed out and they had to carry me away and into the car.

We proceeded to the gravesite to bury Brandon. I was so broken and too far out there that I didn't even know what was being said at his funeral service. When the casket was closed there was too much finality. I had shut down after this so that I didn't have to acknowledge anymore of my loss. Afterwards the church I was attending had a banquet type spread set up for the people who attended the funeral, but I arrived so very late I didn't get to see anyone really. The only person I remember seeing was my childhood friend and then I went back home.

I know that even as tremendously horrible as this incident was I could still see Gods hand at work even when the enemy had tried to destroy my life and make me give up on God. Some evidences of how I knew God had divinely intervened was that the fire never came near my son to burn any part of his body. The fire had completely stopped in a circular curved pattern right in front of the room where he was found and nothing around him was touched by the fire. It indicated to me that he was being protected from the flames. Someone was standing supernaturally in front of that room and was protecting his body. God knew I had never properly said goodbye to Brandon and He knew I would need to see my child one more time face to face to kiss him and hug him goodbye.

I believe that supernatural things were happening while my son was leaving the earth. I honestly believe that Jesus came for my son before he even knew what was happening. Why do I believe that? Because He is a good God and a loving one. In the bible, Jesus says to suffer not the little children and let them come to Him because such is the Kingdom of God. I don't believe God would allow any child to feel the sufferings of death in this life. I believe He meets them upon death and lovingly takes them into His arms.

Later, I found out that my friend saw a vision of two Angels standing with my son together beside his casket. My mother said she saw my son after he died on her favorite rocking chair just sitting there and glowing. I know that my son is safe, and he is not in any danger from anything this world should offer. He will never be sick or hurt again from life and I know I will join him again someday forever in the after-life. It's a promise that I keep dear and near to my heart.

In my attempts to heal and make a difference for my son's life that was so abruptly taken I returned to the scene of the place where he was taken to Heaven. I was determined to find the reason that this happened. Not to point the blame or accuse but to understand why? I didn't question God about it either, just man. I gathered up some of my son's belongings that were left untouched by the fire. It stunk so bad from the smoke that it took me many years before I could be around a fire or even the smell.

Grieving is a process and not everyone does it in the same manner. The mind is stronger than we think and so are our hearts. The problem is that when hope is lost so is life. I honestly can say that without God I would not be here right now. He will always rescue us from the interrupted plans coming from the enemy. He will turn mourning into dancing in time and He will never leave you or forsake you. He does turn ashes into beauty, but you must let him. This is paramount to your healing!

Lesson Learned: It has been sixteen years now since he has been gone. He would have been twenty-three as I publish this book. I still miss him and think of him every day. At times, I will have dreams with him in it and of me being his Mommy. God knows how to comfort us. I realize that he is not coming to me again, but I must go to see him, and it will be for all eternity. I have resolved that in my heart and mind. I hold onto that very promise. As I went through the healing process I was still broken on certain days because I knew I would never get to see him go to his first prom or graduate. Nor would I see him drive his first car or have his own children or even get to see what he would have become in this life. Now I am just grateful that I will see Brandon again and this time it will be forever! It seems like yesterday that he was here and then forever since he has left us all at the same time. The pain subsides but it never fully leaves. The memories are there, and we can talk about him and look at pictures remembering the good times. God still has a plan for me and my younger son that is why were still here. He is not finished with us yet. Or you! When I realized that my younger son was still with me I knew I had to go on. I had to continue to raise this little boy into a man and that all is not lost. This life is still going on and I need to catch up with it for his sake if nothing else. God left us here together so it's up to us to find out why! We must see through the darkness by being led in the Light. We must surface to the top again so that we can catch our breath to see what comes next. If we are still alive and living on this Earth, then that means God is certainly not finished with us yet. That is what we must come to terms with, what is coming next for my life? What may be next for you may be different for what came next for my life. The point is that you must seek it out. In doing so we must leave behind any baggage that came with our situation. Baggage that is disappointment or grief or especially forgiveness. We must find that golden key if you will to help with the solution to move forward. Trust me it won't just be handed to you. It will take everything in you to do this, but it is so crucial to the healing process. I could have easily blamed so many people for this incident and pointed the finger at whoever I wanted to because I was hurt but God told me not to do that. I am not saying that it was an easy thing not to do but when God truly speaks to your heart you will know it's Him speaking and He will provide the peace to ease the pain. My estranged husband was there that night at my work asking me if he should go and pick up the kids and take them home. I told him that I needed to get some milk and bread and he said he was very tired and didn't want to wait for me to get home because he thought I might be longer than he wanted to stay. He did stop by my mom's apartment, saw the kids, and left. My mother was just down a couple of apartments. She could have just kept my son there with her. She didn't have to let him go back to her apartment that night while she stayed and celebrated her friend's birthday. My cousin felt bad and said he should have never dropped off my son because this wouldn't have happened. The truth is that it did and no matter how we try to justify it in our minds who could have done what or who didn't do this or that, it will never change the outcome. No one wins in the blame game. I could have even blamed myself for my relationship being bad with my estranged husband and because of that my kids could have been home if we just got along. The list could go on and on. The reality is that it's over with already. God told me, you must forgive, so that this type of thinking didn't start to seep into my mind. The enemy likes to bring the worst possible scenarios to our life and then pile things on top of it even more so that we will utterly and completely give up on ourselves and God. But I know that I heard God speak to me and I obeyed His voice. We must listen to that inner voice as it speaks to us. It guides us. If I didn't allow God to speak into my life, I could to this day be riddled with guilt and be in a mental institution because on the day of the fire I didn't know that I would never see Brandon again. It was just another ordinary day. I dropped off my younger son to my mother's apartment and when I arrived she was outside. I said where's Brandon? She said, "upstairs he was really tired, and he is probably sleeping because they were up all night playing video games." So, I left without going up to see him and kiss and hug him. I just assumed that I would pick him up after work like I always did. It never happened that way. I never got to say goodbye or give him that one last kiss. There is no one and everyone to blame. In the end, God had the final say. Tomorrow is not promised my friends. It's so important that you not only forgive others, but you must forgive yourself as well. If this is you and you find yourself in the same situation and your struggling, please take a moment to hear God speak. Don't ignore that inner voice. He will show you how to heal from your pain. He will stay with you and bring you through. If he didn't supernaturally talk to me and heal me I couldn't be here sharing with you how to do the same. He's real my friends trust Him.

John 16:33 – I have told you all this so that you may have peace in Me. Here on Earth you will have many trials and sorrows. But take heart, because I have overcome the world.

God will use situations in our lives and He will make all things work together for our good. I want to share with you a little bit about my heart. I have always loved helping people. Before my son's passing I used to feed the next-door neighbors. They lived next to us in a boarding house. Thanks to my mom who always cooked for an army there was plenty of food left over. I would either give away food or give my used clothing away when I wasn't wearing it anymore. If I bought a new piece of clothing I would donate something I hadn't worn in a while. I would always give away the unused toys that my children had outgrown or weren't playing with anymore. I always gave no matter how much I struggled with not having things because I knew what that felt like not to have stuff. After the bills, rent and tithes to the church were taken out we usually had nothing left over. I would live off ten dollars a week. I could not go out with friends or do extra activities with my kids because it wasn't in the budget. We were so blessed to have good landlords at the time because they were always so understanding. When the rent was not paid in full until the following week they always gave us grace.

Because I always gave things or stuff away, I was using a principal in the Word of God and it was operating in my life on a regular basis. The Bible says give and it shall be given to you. What you sow you will reap. Seek the kingdom of God first and all these things will be added unto you. Even with all the hardships in my life we never went without, food, shelter, or clothing. I also started to support a needy child through a sponsorship program that I thought my son Brandon would be a pen-pal with as he grew up but of course that didn't happen, but I continued to support this child from age six until he was eighteen years old. I made a commitment to this child that I would support him until he reached adulthood because I wanted him to have a better life. I promised that I would invest in this poverty-stricken child's life even if we couldn't afford it. Doing all of this was culminating up to something. I just didn't know what?

One night I had a dream that I shared with only a few people and I believe that dream came true in my life as God was preparing me but back then I couldn't understand it. In this dream, I saw myself inside this building of some sorts, it was huge, and I was going through a maze-like formation while walking around in it. As I was looking at things I wasn't walking straight through the building. It was like what you would see in a museum or at an art gallery where you go from one thing to the next. There were pictures laid out on the red drapery used as decoration that covered the tables that were connected. I remember seeing blood. Although the blood wasn't gruesome, it was weird. It was like the dream was trying to reveal a story to me as I passed by each picture, it was like a domino effect as I looked at all the stuff one by one. I seemed to be going upwards as you would a winding staircase to a castle to get to the top of it.

I believe I saw my son's blood and picture amongst the others like a fingerprint sort of. Then I remember running with my son whose body was lifeless and motionless in my arms and carrying him to the top of this building. I got to the top and then I believe my son in his weakness came to me and hugged me. God will always try to speak to us in a way that we can listen. I just wasn't equipped in my walk with Him to pray it through and understand what the dream meant. It was a warning dream. Many years later now I understand what these things mean, and I have learned to pray against anything that does not promote life. Through my son's passing The Brandon House was birthed. It was meant to give back life to others.

One day I saw a vacant building down the street from our home for rent as I walked to the bus stop to get my younger son from the school bus. I just knew that somehow God wanted to use it for the dreams he put in me to make a difference in my city. He was speaking to my heart and I was listening. It took a little bit to get it up and going because the city wasn't sure if they wanted to give me permission for this sort of thing, but God is much bigger than man's mind. I had favor with God and man and so the building was to be called The Brandon House. We signed the papers and took that old building and fixed it up and painted it. It was just a store front building with rooms for rent in the back. I had the permission from my Pastor to hold bible studies there and with the donations from the church and friends I could distribute canned goods and used clothing to the community.

A woman from the church came to help paint the logo on the storefront window. God had it all worked out. I had so much clothing to give away that I didn't know what to do with it all. Tons of baby clothes and adult clothes. We never had a shortage of canned and packaged goods either. God was truly blessing it. Kids were getting saved and adults. The Brandon House was a not for profit ministry that was named after my son who could keep giving after he had left us. It was used for people who needed food, clothing, and encouragement. At times, we prepared meals for the Holidays for those who had no one to share it with. I believe this is one of the reasons that I was always helping people in the neighborhood before this happened, to prepare me for what was coming.

We were in the building for almost a year and doing well until my ex-husband and I started having marital problems. Then he moved into the building with a friend and was backsliding in his walk with God. He went back to his old lifestyle. Then he had my name taken off the lease of the building and had put someone else's name on it. I could not take it any longer. I was crushed that he could even do this after all that had just happened to us. I heard God say lay it down for now and I will allow you to pick it up again one day. As much as it brought me great pain to shut it down I obeyed God and did as He told me.

Looking back in hindsight I know that my son's death was not in vain. Even after shutting the Brandon House down. I had to continue to realize that beyond that, life still has meaning to it if you are still here on this earth. There is no time to give up on the dreams God has placed in your heart or on yourself. You must trust that things will work for the good, for you and your family. Though heartache takes place, love trumps all things. I did rent the building by the grace of God. I ran the ministry to help people, I had my Pastor's covering and my friends came to help. God taught me how to heal amidst the pain through giving back and serving others. It's not about us really. It's about becoming the best person you can be no matter how hard life knocks you down. People were helped and blessed and that's what mattered. The enemy didn't win! Even when he tried his hardest to destroy me by the death of my son and a failing marriage. God is bigger than these temporary things that happen in this lifetime. We must think about the daily day to day operations. We can't go further than that. Worrying is a waste of time. Praying is the preparation for victory.

Community, friends, and family all coming together to make a difference is where the real healing takes place in all of us. We can't change the whole world, but we can help one person at a time. I am so grateful to the people that were a part of my life at the time of this devastating situation because they prayed for me, fed my family, helped with anything that they could. I want to personally acknowledge everyone who had a part in making my life a little easier during this time and say thank you. You will never know how much of an impact you made on my life. I pray even now that Jesus will reward you for all your efforts and love you showed to bless my life during this time.

Today I am stronger than ever, and I am available through this book and my life to be a witness and testimony of God as to how He can restore the broken things and make beauty from ashes.

Lesson Learned: Yes, tragedy is permanent, but grief is not. God is in the business of turning bad situations into something good for yours and my benefit. He is not absent to our pain and grief. He is very much acquainted with affliction and pain. He Himself suffered on the cross even unto death. He understood that His death would solve a problem. He is looking to bring good into the world. That is why He conquered death. There is no condemnation in Him and there is no fear in death, what there is, is life abundant, a God kind of life. God is a God of turn-arounds. He will give you opportunities to find peace and solace during terrible situations. He will teach you lessons you have never learned before and He will show you things in a new light so that you can have a different perspective on how you view a situation. He will show you how to deal with life's trials through His eyes, so you can get a better understanding of how things truly operate and how to bring change and solutions to desperate situations. To the people who have lost hope, love, or someone in their lives, He will comfort you through these trials so that you can comfort others and so that you may know that what happens to you is not in vain. He will use you as a mentor and a teacher to bring others out of heartache, misery, and pain. He will teach you the true path of love. I have learned that God is for me and not against me. This world is going to pass away one day and so am I but in the meantime what I have gained, I want to share with you. Ask yourself what have I done to make a difference in this lifetime? I matter, you matter, we all matter. One person at a time helping another person sets off a chain reaction that leads to someone else learning or comforting another and it brings light into a dark place. It breaks chains of silence and bondages of defeat. If we remain broken and in the dark not only are we missing the rest of our lives and our families lives, we also cannot give from what we refuse to embrace away to others who need our help. It isn't about us, is it? We need to show them the way out of darkness to the One who has all the answers. The One who can solve all our problems, if we will let Him turn the bad things in our lives into something good. Did you know that because God is a problem solver that He can use you to be someone's answer? God took you through your journey and me through my journey so that we could know the depths of heartache and yet have an answer to a better way. You are the answer for someone that is desperately seeking help. You can be their solution. People say all the time that they want to be used by God but for that to happen we must have learned something to give away to others. We must heal and be willing to be available to be that person. We must heal our grief so that others may know how to get through it as well. God is the one who will teach us how to do that. We must trust His process for our lives. Sometimes we must look a little into our future, past all the pain and trauma so that we can see that strength is awaiting our arrival. All we must do is give ourselves a chance. Nothing is wasted in this lifetime, not pain, not death or heartache. These things can bring us closer to understanding our own emotions and those of others. We become that better person that we have always tried to attain to become through our growth process. If we don't eliminate grief, there is no process and we won't get well. We don't see the beautiful opportunities that are waiting for us on the horizon because we have let down the anchor to hold us down at the darkest part of our life. Yet the sun will still come up every day even if you're not awake to see it. The sun will still be there. You must allow yourself to show up! Enjoy the beauty of each day. It was created just for you. Take control of your life and don't let your emotions rule you. You're the commander of your day. You dictate how you will feel. Not your present condition. So, give yourself the chance to see that the grass is greener on the other side because your about to step on over there and take care of it! Give yourself the permission to get free. No one can remove those cumbersome burdens off your life but you. Now I want you to start to strip away any negative things that stand in the way of your emotional healing. I want you to list those negative things and then I want you to command those things to disappear from your life, NOW! Then I want you to take a deep breath and write down what you're never going to give into again that causes you to be emotionally drained. Then tell yourself that God has bought your freedom at a price and that you're fully accepting it for your life.

Ephesians 3:20-21 – Now all glory to God, who is able, through His mighty power at work within us, to accomplish infinitely more than we might ask or think. 21- Glory to Him in the church and in Christ Jesus through all generations forever and ever, Amen!

Chapter 11- The Divorce

Let's go backwards now to my love life as a Christian woman. I had never been married before and I was looking forward to the day when I was. I don't think I understood all that a marriage entailed, like so much hard work or what it meant to struggle if you were married to the wrong person, but I found out the hard way very quickly. I think I had a different version in my mind of what I thought marriage was. My version was that marriage consisted of one big happy family where two people deeply loved each other and coexisted in peace and harmony. Doesn't sound bad, does it? It sounds ideal. The reality about my first marriage was that it wasn't anything that I describe above.

I was a one-man woman now. Cheating for me was not an option. I believed in sex after marriage and I was sober. I was moving forward but in the wrong direction concerning my love life. I am going to be completely honest with you as I said I would be. You will read it as I lived it and I am not holding anything back on this subject matter. My purpose is to be transparent so that you may not have to go through the same things that I have gone through.

The problem I had with my ex in the beginning was that we were spending too much time alone together without any people being around us. How many know the flesh is so weak and self-serving? There was no one to stop us or tell us that we were taking it too far. When the flesh takes over God seems to be removed for the moment. We progressed from one stage to the next until we had made sexual contact. This is what I think was the main attraction between us in the first place. Two lonely people who have been hurt in relationships but still wanted that special love from someone.

Although I wanted someone responsible and who could take the initiative to handle a family, I didn't take the time to get to know all the details about his life, so when the sex finally happened everything that I was supposed to find out about him in the process took a back seat. Don't judge someone by their outward appearances only because there can be much deeper issues on the inside of them that you have no clue about. I didn't take the time to find out more about him. I just let my emotions take me to places that they shouldn't have gone. Then when I did see signs along the way that were evident of past failed relationships and I recognized that I didn't want that again, it was too late, I had already given my body to him.

I was so wrapped up in my emotions at this point and that is what the whole relationship was based on, emotions, not true love. I recall him lying to me so many times and even though I knew in my heart that this whole relationship was wrong, I did not cut him off from my life. This relationship certainly wasn't based on any godly character or decisions. Somehow, he kept wooing me with charm, flowers, a bended knee, and heartfelt words of "I won't ever do it again." He would write me poems and call me his "special lady" and I admit it made me feel like I was the only woman in the world who was loved by him. Who could resist this kind of charisma?

Even as I saw the wrong things being done in the relationship and towards me, I still married him. I did try to break it off, but his charm worked every time. I was new to it. It was believable at the time. His mother had just passed, and things were emotional for us already. In a matter of months, I had destroyed all that I had preserved. I didn't fall back into drugs or alcohol, but I was betraying myself by cutting my options off from the true King coming to me by accepting a frog instead.

People can seem to be charming, yet they are deceiving at the same time. He seemed to have it all together. He was working and had his own apartment. He seemed like a good dad and appeared to be marriage material. When I started to get to know him we were already married. He came from a dysfunctional family who struggled with drugs and alcohol. Then he himself became involved in the very same things. It caused him to become dysfunctional. Then he built his own family and that had its share of problems. It left his children without a father figure and leadership in the home. This then spilled over into our extended family causing more dysfunction to evolve in our home.

It was a huge strain on the marriage. There was broken trust and the love was quickly fading. There was so much mental and physical abuse. The police officers were called constantly. I would move out for a while with our kids. Then move back in. It became too much to handle. I was so frustrated because I was trying to be this godly woman and live for God while the man I was married to went back on drugs and eventually started cheating on me.

One thing remained, I had made a promise to God that when I got married I would not get divorced unless it was because of an adulterous relationship and I kept my word. Even though I was suffering from so much mental abuse I kept my vows before God. I figured if I kept my word to stay in the marriage that God would work it all out. So just to keep the peace I would go out when he was home so that there were less arguments as possible. There was still great unrest in the home. I started believing that he enjoyed making me upset. At this point I hardly ever laughed. Which was something I loved to do. I was always sad or crying. I eventually realized this isn't the way marriage was supposed to be. This isn't how any relationship should be!

After my son passed, all kinds of emotions started to rise with in my soul. I felt the need to forgive and have everyone who was family stay as close as possible to me. I even asked my ex to move back home after our last separation and he agreed. As I started to heal emotionally from my son's death I saw that my relationship with my ex was not going to work no matter how much I forgave him. I started to notice big changes in him.

So, while he was living in the building that was called The Brandon House, I heard God speak so clearly, He told me to shut the ministry down. I freely gave up the building for God because I wasn't going to let him embarrass God's name by bringing drugs and strangers in there. He knew that I had it at this point and he eventually went to our Pastor and finally confessed to him about what had really been going on in his life. It was a private conversation between the two of them.

I decided to give it one more chance because there was no infidelity that I knew of up until this point. But something deep in my spirit was tugging at my heart and letting me know that there was more to the story. I knew there was something else going on, but I could not prove it. I got scolded by him for checking his phone bill that had unknown phone numbers on it. He would start to make up excuses that he had to go out and do estimates at odd times of the day and night. He would even use his ex as an excuse saying he had to go over to her house to fix something. He would decline sex and his behavior was different and erratic. I didn't even know who he was anymore.

Finally, I acted on my instincts and I called our Pastor and told him something still isn't right. The Pastor said didn't he tell you the whole story? I replied no. He then said that he would call him so that he would have to tell me the whole story about what he was still doing. I agreed to meet him at one of his daughter's house that same night and he told me all that my heart was already telling me. That he had been cheating but for five months. That was the last straw for me. The worst of it all was the betrayal.

Right before we had this conversation about him cheating on me and using drugs, I was standing by him and was still willing to support him while he got help for the drug abuse. The day before I found out about him cheating on me I decided to pick him up from where he was living and bring him home. I planned a day just for us to show him that I was willing to make the marriage work. We had an intimate time together and the very next day I found out that he was cheating on me. I was sick to my stomach.

After he finally told me the whole truth about what happened I composed myself as I left his daughters house and I drove home. I ran up the stairs and into the shower as fast as I could, and I continuously scrubbed my body. I literally felt like I was violated. It was one of the worst feelings. I felt filthy and used. I was so emotionally drained at this point that I crawled into my bed and I cried for hours.

Then, through all the tears I heard the Lord speak to me so clearly and He said, "I have already divorced him from you", you have a choice now to divorce him yourself. I told the Lord I choose divorce. That was all I needed, was to hear from God. From that moment forward my decision was made, it was biblical and final. There was no guilt in ending the very thing that guilt made me do. I had one last question to ask him, so I could have closure and that was, why didn't you tell me the whole truth? He said to me, "that he was taking that part to the grave because he knew I would divorce him over it".

In all the years that we were together he was right about one thing, I would divorce him for cheating on me because of all the lies. That spring I laboriously studied on how to properly do paperwork for a divorce. I couldn't afford a lawyer. I spent lots of hours and days in front of a computer at my local library. Eventually, with a lot of prayer, faith, and God's help, I was granted a divorce that summer and it was finally over.

Lesson Learned: Boundaries, need I say more? O my goodness some people must have them. I think it is a sign of respect to consider one's boundaries. I also believe that if you truly love someone you will let them cross over into your boundaries in a healthy way. It's like a two-sided coin. There can be healthy and unhealthy boundaries that co-exist in a relationship. Healthy boundaries are easier to adapt to and most people don't argue over them or feel bad if the line is crossed. But unhealthy boundaries cause division and make you feel bad after you cross them. Examples of unhealthy boundaries are when you allow someone to walk all over you or you continue to allow some form of abuse to happen in your relationships. Whether it's mental or physical. Some people have no boundaries at all and anything goes. We all at one time or another are led by these types of boundaries. I started out with healthy boundaries by getting sober and abstaining from sex until I met the wrong partner. He had no boundaries. So, there was nothing to work with. Then I switched over to unhealthy boundaries by giving in to having sex with him. I was starting to compromise my walk with God and it was bothering me. At first, I thought well maybe this is my real chance at true love for once. But I was not waiting long enough to let God redirect me. I knew better. My flesh wanted love that's all. I had no one to blame but myself. This caused me to start living with unhealthy boundaries and I made a mess of my life for a certain amount of years because of it. It took many years to put my life back together again because of my bad choices. I had to re-learn how to receive genuine love and how to laugh again due to all the pain and trauma that I had endured. I'm not stupid but I knew from the beginning that he wasn't the right man for me. He had issues and the signs were all there. But I wanted to be a wife and have a family. So, I compromised. I thought well one day we will see the breakthrough, but that day never came. I endured him lying, making excuses, and running his life like he was single because I loved his kids and my kids loved his kids. It was hard to separate us at this point. I also made a covenant with God when I decided to get married to this person, that I wouldn't divorce him unless there was infidelity in the marriage. These were the reasons I kept taking him back. At this point I was so drained and weak after losing my son and then giving up The Brandon House building due to his drug abuse that I just gave in. The only thing I could do was cry day after day and pray to God. I kept taking him back because I trusted that God would somehow give me a solution to this mess that I got myself into. A solution did come but not in the way I expected it to. So, by marital infidelity, I no longer biblically was mandated to stay with this man anymore and I chose divorce. Now I might get some slack here because people will say, God hates divorce. Yes, He does. But I believe he hates abuse too. I kept my end of the deal with God until the release came. I tried everything that I knew to do to help the marriage work and it wasn't working at all. All you can do is make peace with men if possible, Gods word says. This is exactly what I was doing. Could I have stayed with him through the infidelity? Sure. The problem was this relationship was never based on genuine love but lies, deceit and bad choices. All the counseling never helped one bit and you can't change anyone, only God can if their willing to let Him change them. Do I regret my decision to divorce him? No. Did I get upset because of the divorce? Of course, it was painful. When you've spent so many years with someone even if it was traumatic you get used to them being around. Who knows what would have happened if it was only a one-night stand or there was no cheating at all going on? The point here is that through it all God has healed me, and I have forgiven him. I pray the best for him and that he doesn't miss Heaven. If you are in this kind of situation or have ever been, please know that forgiveness is a powerful tool for healing your heart. People are dysfunctional they have problems some people never get the solution to their problem because they never address their issues. Take some time out today to see what issues may be hindering you from having an abundant life. Forget about the past it is never coming back. Look ahead! Your worth it. Take the time to see if you need to create some healthy boundaries for you or someone that is crossing the line. It is sometimes a matter of life or death, health, and stress. It can all be avoided when we realize there are certain behaviors that we don't have to accept when we see the red flags! Take inventory today. Stop what you're doing and reflect on your current relationships. If you see something that is affecting your life negatively you have the power within you to make the necessary changes. So, start the process now. You will thank yourself for the unnecessary heartache overall. Trust me!

Hebrews 13:4 – Marriage should be honored by all, and the marriage bed kept pure, for God will judge the adulterer and all the sexually immoral.

Chapter 12- Becoming a Single Everything

Here I was this newly divorced woman and a single mother with a one-person income. I can't lie the freedom from the marriage was a huge weight off my shoulders, but it did not come without a price to pay. I was relieved that I was divorced but I must say the emotional struggle of having to go through divorce is not easy. Having to relive all the mental and physical abuse all over again was draining. But I made it through that ugly season of my life.

For me, I was now taking the time to get emotionally, spiritually, and physically built back up. I was focusing on my younger son and his emotional wellbeing. Now that my ex and I no longer functioned as a unit, I had become the sole provider. He only had supervised visitations with our son due to his drug habit. He started coming out on the days he was supposed to for a brief period. Then eventually he started to do "no shows" by calling his son and telling him that he couldn't make his visit on that day. Eventually, he wouldn't call or show up at all and I was the one who had to watch our son cry repeatedly. It was heart-breaking!

I found that if I didn't properly handle my emotions and go through the process with God about how I was feeling concerning the whole situation that I would be fatigued and stressed out all the time because I was allowing the situation to rule my life. You've heard that stress can kill, right? I felt like I was dying slowly from it. Although friends and church people are great to have to talk and pray with, nothing is better than the relationship I have with God. He truly was my only trust worthy friend, especially during my distress. I could anchor my soul in Him safely.

After getting myself together again I was ready to move forward with the peace of God. The only thing that kept me grounded was my faith. I went back to work and started to pick up the pieces one by one that were left undone. I continued to go to church. I tried to catch up with all the debt that I was left with, but it was difficult. Debt collectors were calling and threatening me every day. It was extremely difficult managing a home with a child all alone. I had to take on several jobs to help make ends meet.

I remained single because thinking about getting into any relationship at the time was the furthest thing from my mind. So, I enrolled into college. I went for two years. I kept my mind occupied as I walked through the healing process that only God could have helped me with. I didn't know of anyone else who I could personally relate my story to who had lost a child and then got divorced shortly afterwards. It's not something that is a common thing in people's lives to have happen all at once. Yet, not having that someone to hold me or just listen to me made it difficult while I not only grieved my son but also the loss of my marriage.

I found out that the next best thing to do was to stay busy. I can only thank God for keeping my sanity intact while I temporarily exited this crazy rollercoaster that I was on. I had no choice but to be a single mother who wasn't going to give up or admit defeat. It wasn't who I was regardless of all the trauma that I was going through. So, I toughed it out.

Summer was over, and my younger son went back to school. Things were returning to as normal as they could possibly be. I tried to make our home a safe place again after all the loss that we had gone through. Life's circumstances can teach you so much if you allow it to. You can either give up the reigns or take your experiences and put them to good use. Life has many lessons to teach you whether they are good or bad ones but as with anything if you're not willing to learn from them then you will remain a bitter or angry person from it.

I have had many such instances of where I could have allowed life's lessons to destroy me but because I recognized that I have "the choice" to choose which way life could go, I made the choice to take the higher road. I could have literally been put in the Looney bin if I would have chosen the lower road. It took everything in me to wake up every morning and put one foot in front of the other and to make it through the day. It wasn't always easy. There were a lot of hidden tears from my family and friends.

In the process of grieving I also had to undo things that my ex did to destroy me by lying to our Pastor at the time about my character. He taped me once cursing during an argument. It was after he tormented me, but he didn't tape that part. I never knew that he had did that until years later. Someone from the church told me the truth about what he did. I couldn't understand why for the longest time that I was being tested and put on probation periods in my church, where I served faithfully, before I could be in any leadership positions. I thought that I was just being put on the back burner.

When the truth finally came out that my ex had lied, things started to change within the church and my character was restored. Here it took the end of our relationship to prove that it wasn't me doing the damage, yet I was falsely being accused in the meantime. It seemed like it would never end. I was constantly fixing one thing or another. There was so much damage done from this relationship.

I do take full blame for being an angry woman in the relationship but not for the abuse. I have forgiven my ex. I don't want to live with regrets or un-forgiveness. One thing that all of this did lead me to realize was that my relationships in my church and with other people were not always what I thought they were.

I had family and friends that helped me through some of my grief and I did feel the love from everyone and even from strangers that I had never even met during my unforeseen circumstances. Yet, I still found life to be so difficult. Raising my son alone while still attending church was a lonely experience. Few males stepped up to help nurture my son during the times when he needed a male figure in his life. I must be honest here, at one point because of those types of experiences I seriously thought that it didn't matter if they stepped up to help me and that by me being both mom and dad that there wouldn't be any difference in it influencing my son. I thought that I in and of myself would be able to give him enough to compensate for being both the mom and dad, but I was wrong.

In my mind, I thought that the church I was attending at the time would help to mentor my son beings he had not only lost his brother but also his father who was absent from his life. The sad fact is that it didn't happen that way. Most of the families in the church both had two parents. Those children seemed to be favored more so than the single kids. I noticed that early on when some of the men in the church would correct my son for running around or goofing off, because inside of him was lacking that male figure, they would scold him instead of loving on him or being a father figure to him. They didn't do that with the two parent families. Couldn't they see that my son needed love instead of criticism? The Pastor at one point asked me if my son had the normal activities of school life and such. I couldn't believe some of the things that were happening to me as a single parent even by people who you thought you could trust and rely on.

Really? That's what I thought. Not only did my son lose his brother but also his grandfather who died in the fire too and his father who was now out of the picture. I wondered how can people be so blind or uncompassionate? I admit I had a difficult time with the church after these things. There were people in the church who pushed my son away in subtle ways. Like when certain kids were going over someone's house and my son wasn't invited. Little things like this used to upset me.

During the many years that I dealt with this problem I had known more about the criticism that was being spoken than the criticizers knew that I was aware of. I got to see who my true friends were at the time and guess what there weren't many. It makes you wonder who can you trust in your deepest time of need? I learned how to separate the fakes. Eventually, I was put on staff at my church where I got paid. I cleaned the church and then moved up to the secretary of the Pastor. Until about a year later when he let me go because he said they needed my yearly salary for their budget to redesign the churches bathrooms. At this point I couldn't believe it. Bathrooms? Instead of giving a single parent a job? What happened to taking care of the orphans and the widows like the bible says? I wasn't the only person hurt in the church. Several people had left before me and now I was just waiting for the time that I would be leaving too. At least God used them to employ me. Which I was grateful for.

Single parenting is never an easy position to be in. You must wear so many hats. You had to be both mother and father at the same time on the same day. You must be the bread-winner, the sports coach, the bedtime story-reader, etc.... The list is a mile long. I was worn out like an old shoe needing repairs. Yet I never gave up. This was my only son left and I was going to make sure if anyone was there for him to depend on it was going to be me. I would never abandon him.

Now it just wasn't in the church that I saw the single parent syndrome at work, but it also happened when he played sports. I noticed that the coaches didn't favor him because he wasn't experienced at the sport he was in. But how would I have found the time for that too? Yet, they didn't ask to coach him on off days. I took him to every practice and went to all his games, but I couldn't mentor him the way a dad could in this area.

I had to sit by and watch my son's desire to have that one on one fellowship with a male figure not happen. It broke my heart. The point is people looked at my son who was a child with issues instead of pouring love into him and bringing out the best in him. Instead they criticized and pushed him to the side as if he was a problem child. When the truth was, he was, a hurting child seeking love. Granted my son at times was rowdy but look at what he just went through. It just goes to show it doesn't take a village to raise a child, it takes two parents!

Lesson Learned: No one wakes up one morning and says hey, let's get divorced because I want to be a single parent, right? No, we don't. Most of the time we are put in positions that cause us to become one. There is no parental handbook for when the baby comes or a systematic guide on how to care for your baby. It's the same thing with being a single parent you must manage the situation as you go along on the journey. It's another facet of life that can bring great stress in our lives. The real key here is to have the faith to believe that God is who He says He is and to watch Him work those everyday miracles out as we stay obedient to His will. His will is that we wouldn't cave in or give up. His will is that we stay the course because those little ones need us. They need our guidance and protection. Your children themselves will need healing from the other parent being absent in their lives. There are so many dynamics that shift once you become a single parent. It involves court cases and custody battles and division of time. The worst part is if one parent is not fully present due to illness or drug addiction or whatever the case may be, then we as single parents must step it up another notch. When my son turned eighteen I realized as I looked back that I did everything I possibly could to provide and protect my child in the best way I knew how. I felt good about what I did. I felt like my son turned out to be a good kid after all the struggles we have been through and I have no regrets. My only goal was to make sure that my son was a productive member in society and that the choices I made were never his fault. None of it was. I got myself into the situation and it was my job to get me out. That's the real key here, to know how to get out of situations that are not pertinent to your life or your children. Like for example, I didn't rush into any relationships because I realized that raising my son was more important and that he needed me 100 percent of the time, beings I had to be two parents at once. Structure in the home is so important. Children need that. I realized that I didn't want to get involved in any relationships while he was little because number one I didn't want another broken heart and two he didn't need someone else to leave his life again. We both needed healing in our hearts from all the trauma and loss. It's important that we stop and examine ourselves. We should see where we may be putting up road blocks to our or our children's progress. I did all that I could to make ends meet with material and monetary means. I must say, in all honesty I now see how important it is to have two parents raising children. They need that stability of both a man and a woman. They need the different ways that each parent loves so that their little hearts aren't void of the roles that are involved in the family unit. That's why a lot of us cannot receive our healing because somewhere we have been void of a certain kind of love. I find it no coincidence that God who calls Himself ABBA (father) is a father to the orphan. It is more common that males leave or are absent from the family unit than the mother is, and God has literally stepped into that position so that people may know that they are never fatherless. How beautiful is that? God is also our husband ladies. He is a sustainer and if we believe that with our whole hearts He will provide for us. He loves children and would never want to see anything evil happen to them. He is the missing piece to the single parent situation. He is that very thing we need to help us in our income, emotions, relationships, etc. If we have Him, then we have all we need! If your feeling so desperately lonely let Him fill your life with His love and let Him give you the things that no one else can. Look at your life and see what area is lacking because there isn't another parent there. Then write it down and pray over that missing link for 14 days. I dare you to watch God move on your behalf! Keep yourself busy and make every day count. Start doing things in your life that make you happy as if it was your last day on Earth. You only get this one life, so don't forget that!

Joshua 1:9 – This is my command, be strong and courageous! Do not be afraid or discouraged. For the Lord, your God is with you wherever you go.

Chapter 13- Moving to Florida
(leaving the past behind)

I decided to move to Florida! A long-time desire prompted my decision to want to go to bible school. One month some visitors from another ministry came to do a conference at the church where I was attending. I was so moved by the impact of the ministry during the time they were with us that I felt God say, if there came a chance for me to go and get schooling with their bible college that I should go. The name of the college was called Zoë. I thought wow my prayers to leave this crazy part of my life behind were all starting to get answered. I had received some money from a settlement that had taken many years to finally end. I received a portion of the money and had decided that for the best interest in my son's life and mine that we should move and go where God instructed me to go. Which happened to be Florida. I decided to pursue an application from Zoe college and then I mailed it back to them. Finally, I could afford it and so when I had received the phone call that I was accepted I started preparing to move.

It was a huge decision that I had to make but I wanted to do it. I had to pack up as much as I could as a single parent with my son and leave to go to a place that I didn't know anything about. It meant leaving everyone and everything behind, but I knew at the time that it was exactly what my son and I needed. I wouldn't call it running away as much as needing some time to separate from the pain and heartache that was going on in both of our lives. We needed to get away from the familiarity of a lifestyle that was filled with bad memories and what seemed to be more depressing than productive. I couldn't stand watching my son cry repeatedly because his father didn't show up for his visits with his son. That made the decision easier to make to leave for Florida. We needed to breathe again, and God was providing an opportunity for us to do just that.

I started putting all my affairs in order. I first had to get out of debt from all the unpaid bills that my ex-husband didn't pay. From home expense bills to all the maxed-out credit cards that were run up when he didn't work or was blowing his money on drugs. I used to have to put everything on charge cards when we were married, bills, food, clothing, gas, you name it I charged it. He had bad credit, so all the cards had to go in my name or we couldn't get credit cards.

Instead of being bitter about the situation I decided that God had blessed me with the money to get out of debt, so I resolved almost thirty thousand dollars' worth of debt and chose to forgive my ex who put us into that position in the first place. I tried to pay back the people who he owed money to as well. Next, I bought a new truck because the car I had been driving had a blown head gasket and was ready to die at any moment. I wound up giving the car away to someone who needed one. She knew a mechanic who could look at it for her and fix it. Lastly, I paid off all the debt that my mother had, or she would not have been able to move out on her own when we left. I also purchased a mobile home for her and paid her rent for the year, so she could get back on her feet again. She declined to move to Florida with us. Rightfully so, we all suffered and needed to go through this journey to get ourselves on course again and God provided for us to do that through horrific circumstances. But God made the enemy pay me back for what he stole from me.

When my older son and my mother's fiancé passed on she immediately moved in with me and lived with us for five years. Now that we were leaving for Florida she needed a place of her own. It seemed to be a fresh start for everyone. I made sure to bless the ones that I loved by distributing money amongst some of my family members so that they could get ahead and fix their vehicles or go on a trip to visit others. Then we started to pack. Time was of the essence because I had to be in Florida to enroll in school by a certain date. I had to keep everything moving in an orderly fashion. We packed vigorously to get everything cleared out of the old house so that nothing was left behind.

God had truly blessed me through this whole process. There were no hindrances. I'm a giver, so I wound up leaving behind a lot of furniture, beds, dressers, a washer, and dryer, etc....I figured everything was in good shape and that these things could bless the future tenants. I also allowed my landlords to keep my security deposit of seven years because they were the kindest people when it was difficult for us to have all our rent money paid on time. They were always patient, and they never charged us late fees. They always showed us grace. I couldn't have asked for better landlords. I wanted to sow something back into their lives as well.

I left before the house was vacated. My family helped my mom transition into her new place. I paid for the moving van and gave them money to move her. I wanted to bless everyone for all their help.

I still remember my son and I heading off with a fully loaded truck. We could only fit our most prized and valuable possessions. It was difficult to say goodbye, but I knew there was an adventure ahead of us that needed to be sought out. It took about two days for us to arrive in Florida because we wanted to take our time getting there. Before we left I made sure to get my son some electronic games to keep him busy during the long trip. He was such a trooper and a great traveling partner. Finally, we crossed the end of the Georgia state line and there it was the sign that said, Welcome to Florida!

We arrived at our destination. Everything seemed so new and fresh due to the change of scenery. Yet at the same time it all looked very foreign. We didn't have a place to live at yet and I didn't know one thing about the area. I just used my faith and I trusted God fully because I believed this is where the next season of our lives were to take place. Miami Beach is like a world unto itself. I could not find any stores or familiar places that I knew to eat or shop at. It took quite some time to finally check into a hotel that would house us for a couple of weeks until we found a place to live.

Once we settled into the hotel and put our things away we decided to go look for places to get food and toiletries. Finally, I found a Walgreens where we could get some things to hold us over. The very first day after we arrived I got a flat tire. I had all brand-new tires too. I had such a hard time trying to fix the flat because I didn't have the proper tools. I didn't know where a tire place was either. I felt so lost. The people from the hotel were all just watching me from afar trying to change a tire with no success. I couldn't believe no-one had offered to help me! Finally, one guy came over and helped me to get the tire changed. This was my first lesson about Miami Beach, it is all about self!

The next thing that was on the to do list was to look for a place to live. I found out very quickly that if you want things done in Miami Beach you're going to need to do it for yourself. During my travels, I somehow met this real estate man. He was quite young but very polite and more than willing to help me. I know it was God because I had no clue what I was doing. He took me to see a couple of places to live at, but I wasn't interested. I knew my time was running out at the hotel where we were staying at so something had to materialize quickly.

The problem in finding a place to live was that I had no job or references. No one wants to rent to someone who isn't working. But God orchestrated the whole process for us. I wound up renting a condominium that just became available above the real estate place where the guy I met worked. Of course, it didn't come without a price. I had to put two deposits down plus the first month's rent to show good faith so that they would lease the condominium to me. I was so relieved because I needed to find housing for my son, so he could go to school. It was important that I maintained a stable environment in the transition that we were going through.

After getting a place, I finally went to the school to get my fees and classes all taken care of and to find a babysitter. I must say God had my steps ordered from the moment I left my past behind me. There is something that happens when you just believe and act in faith that things will turn out okay. The very first day I arrived at the school God met my need for a babysitter. It just so happened that one of the student's husband was out of work and needed a job.

On that same day that I had gone to the college to enroll I also got to meet the babysitter. We instantly clicked. From that day forward, I never had to worry about childcare again. Things were most certainly falling right into place. I was very generous in the pay I gave for my son's childcare not only because it was needed for both of us but also because I was grateful for the person who took care of my son. My son liked this person and looked up to him. A male figure was missing in my son's life for a long time. An honest male figure to speak good things into his life was exactly what he needed. God surely knew what He was doing. In the beginning, I didn't like the idea of leaving my son with a stranger but it all worked out so wonderfully.

After my older son passed I wouldn't let my younger son stay with anyone. Those feelings came due to my loss. You go through the strangest process after losing a child that it causes you to act in a very over protective way. But I saw God working in every detail to work all things together for our good, so how could I not walk in faith? I couldn't deny that he had chosen the right person to be in my son's life and I trusted God.

After settling all those issues, I was finally able to move all our over-stuffed trash bags that were filled with clothes and such from my truck into our new place. The only down fall was that we were now living in a high rise. Every time we came in or out we had to take an elevator. It was tiring but exciting at the same time. I didn't have one piece of furniture. Not a couch or beds. I learned how to find stores and places to eat by getting lost. It was so crazy. When I finally found a place to shop we bought air mattresses to sleep on. It took a while to find a furniture store. When I finally found the them, they charged me a fortune for furniture.

All I knew was that we had to get beds. We were constantly blowing up our air mattresses and it was a tedious job. I finally picked out furniture to furnish our condominium. They delivered everything to us. After we got beds and a couch someone finally told me where Target and Wal-Mart were located. That was how I finished the last of the decorating by buying the rest of our things from those stores.

The final steps were to enroll my son into a school and find a new pediatrician for him. In Florida, you must have certain forms filed with the school before they can be enrolled. If you didn't have these two forms your child was not getting into school. I finally found a doctor. Then I had to purchase uniforms for his school. It was strange for my son to wear uniforms because he never had to wear them before. He wasn't happy about it either. I started school and he started school. My son was trying to meet new friends. The area where we moved was a city. There were more Hispanic and Mexican people living in the area. So, he got to meet different cultures of people.

I had some interesting things occur while living in Miami Beach. It was more of a lower-class area that we were living in, but I didn't know that. My son was catching pin worms from the other kids in school. Something we never even knew happened amongst kids. In Jersey, we never heard of pin worms or dealt with anything like that. Then I got them. It was crazy because it happened more than once. Even if you don't have the worms everyone in the family must take the medicine for prevention.

I was so mad when that kept happening to him. My son learned cuss words that he should never have repeated but he didn't know any better. He learned things about sex that I had never discussed with him and he was only seven! The atmosphere was completely different than what we came from. The teachers weren't involved with their children's progress. We didn't remain long in that residence. The neighbor's downstairs were annoying. He would have parties every night and blast his music until 3am. He had his speakers mounted on his walls! Which vibrated up to mine.

Where I lived at the police told me that unless someone is being murdered then you should work it out with the other person. The office didn't help much either. Beings there was no help from either the police or the office I decided to move. I found another place through a person from my school. A teacher there had lead me to a person who was renting their house out. Now mind you in Miami Beach everything costs triple for what you pay for to live there. This rent was not cheap at all. It was double the cost of the condominium. But it was a house with a yard and no elevator and it had a washer and dryer.

For my son's stability, it was so important for me to continue to establish a peaceful environment because of all that we had just been through with our family being torn apart. As a good parent, we do everything we can to make our children's world safe. It was a priority to bring some of that balance back again for him. I was determined to find a suitable and quiet place for us to live. So, I met with this new landlord who also required two deposits. The whole system in Miami Beach was all about the money. That is what makes their world go around! As she took me to the house to walk through it, I found the house to be old and dirty from being unoccupied for a while. It literally looked like no one had lived in it for several years. It had utilities that were out dated, and my washer and dryer was outside. It had the 70's décor on the walls and the tiling in the one bathroom was that baby powder blue color from the 60's. Yet I was so desperate to move that I accepted her offer knowing that I could redecorate. It was right down the street from my school and my sons new school. I furnished it with what I had and a few other things. It was so nice to finally be in a place where it was quiet.

My neighbors were nice. I didn't know the neighbors on the one side of me but the guy on my other side was very kind. He also referred me to his landscaper. They were both Christians and it was nice knowing that I lived next to people who cared. My next-door neighbor also rented out a house from my landlord. My landlord was nice. She would immediately fix things when they broke. Like the air conditioning that kept cutting off. In Florida, you don't want that to happen. We had minor incidents of Palmettos crawling across the floor when you least expected it and there were mice that were coming into the house. I tried to rectify the situation myself, but they were manifesting too much. She did tend to the issues.

Eventually we didn't see that many. I had a fenced in yard and thought it a good idea to introduce a pet into our family. I knew my son didn't have any friends yet, so I thought it would be a good idea to occupy his time with a puppy. The search for a dog was ridiculous. Again, not knowing where to go I wound up at an expensive pet store. We purchased a Shih-Tzu who turned out to have breathing problems, so we took her back to the pet store to be treated for it. It took forever to get her certificate of authenticity. I'm not even sure if it is real.

Shortly after our purchase at the pet shop it closed. So, I had to find our own vet where I could get her up to date with shots. But when we brought her home from the vets she had caught fleas from their office! I was so upset because fleas are so hard to get rid of. Eventually after arduous vacuuming and much flea spray, powder and bombing the house I got rid of the fleas. This was another exciting adventure that took place. It was quite an interesting journey so far might I add.

We had to make the best of it. I wasn't moving anytime soon. This time we lived among the Hasidic Jewish community. They didn't talk to you unless you were buying something in their store and you were not allowed to bring any un-kosher food to their restaurants. One time I was trying to get something to eat at one of their restaurants and my son had a Burger King bag. We were going to sit outside and eat at the tables and the guy came out telling us that my son was not allowed to have that food on their tables. I was upset but respected him and left.

There was only one Jewish man that I had met who would talk to me and he was not of the norm. I was still attending school and things were progressing along. My one friend from my childhood lived in Florida already. She would come to visit us with her kids. My son enjoyed that so much. I was traveling to different places by myself to explore things that I never had the chance to do. My friend would come and stay the weekends with the kids and I would pay her generously for her time and gas to drive to my house. It took a few hours to get from one place to another, so I wanted to be a blessing to her and her family.

After about ten months of attending school I found out that they were changing their hours to the morning time. Which would alleviate the need for a babysitter. The problem with that was, if I was needed during the day for any reason concerning my son's school or had to stay home with him because he was sick it would have made it difficult for me to attend school. I prayed about it and God spoke. He said in two months' time the school will be closing anyhow so disregard any awkward feelings you may have about leaving early. Talk to the dean and tell them your story. So, I left the School.

LESSON LEARNED: Well let me tell you this our move to Florida was quite interesting. I was so full of faith. I was ready for a new chapter to begin in my life. I was done with the familiar. I mean who makes the decision to just pack up all their things and travel to another state with your child and not know a thing about where your moving to? Me. I did just that I took me and my son and all our important belongings and left. Everything about the trip was freeing. Leaving the past behind us was so exhilarating. I had to lean on God for every decision after that. He had provided the money for us to go there and live, so I figured I let Him help with the rest of our transition. We were foreigners in a strange place. It took some time for us to adjust to the living situations, but we did. Everywhere we lived there was a situation that I had to deal with. The one residence that we lived in, our neighbor was loud and noisy, so we had to move. The other place that we moved into was quiet but had bugs and mice. The rent was astronomically high. Yet we still had some type of issue everywhere we lived. At first it was fun because it was new but then it was getting old. What I learned is that you can't run away from your problems. They will remain with you wherever you go. They are attached to your soul. Unless you separate them and heal you can run all you want to, but nothing will change. It's so important that we get a breather, maybe a much-needed vacation or possibly moving to another state is in order. But not without being healed. I thought that the change of scenery would help me to feel better and it did for a while. Eventually we all must face our demons. I had to be real with God. I had to acknowledge that He sees all of me no matter where I try to hide. When those feelings weren't dealt with I was not well. I manifested all types of aches and pains from the stress of denying my healing. I don't know why we do that when God knows all about us and He is more than willing to lend a helping hand. Even when we try to ignore God He is still there wanting to love us. Why do we run from His love? I have learned now that I can turn from any mistake that I have made and run to His loving kindness and He will deliver me. See we must want to be delivered. We should want to come out of the pit that we have put ourselves in and let love overwhelm us. So many of us have been hurt by love, that it causes us not to trust God to love us well enough or in the right way to heal us. His love is unlike any other love. It's supernatural. It defies human logic. It can penetrate those places that a human's love never could. It is a complete redemptive power that invades the hearts of mankind. With that said, don't you want that kind of love in your life? When God spoke to me about going back home I knew somehow that even though things weren't right they were going to be, and I wasn't afraid to let Him love me in my weakness. If I had the faith to leave and go on a natural journey to an unknown place and let God put things in place for me there, why would I not let Him heal me supernaturally in my spirit? So, in this moment as your reading this I want you to realize how precious you are and how much you are loved! Go beyond human reasoning and the way we love and start taking on a new perspective about how God loves. I know that this will revolutionize and change your whole way on how to not only love yourself but how you love others as well. Start finding scriptures right now and pick out a favorite one and mediate on that for one week. Let it resonate in your spirit. Let it speak life into your soul so that you never run or hide away from anyone or anything ever again, especially God! Be vulnerable with yourself because God will never hurt you He will love and heal you.

Ephesians 2:10 – For we are God's masterpiece. He has created us anew in Christ Jesus, so we can do the good things He planned for us long ago.

Chapter 14- Be Careful Who You Trust!

My greatest joy is to be a blessing to people. I'm a giver and not selfish at all. I've been told that I care too much, is that possible? Where ever there is a need that I can meet, I will do my best to meet that need. I helped a lot of people while living in Florida not to mention family members, my own friends, and ministries. I had the means to do it. So, I did. I made some awesome friends and some that betrayed me along the way. Living in Miami Beach was overwhelming for both my son and me. It was time for us to leave that area, but I wanted to stay in Florida because I loved it there. So, we started to search in an area where my friend lived so that we could be closer to her and her family. She was always asking me to come live there anyway over the years.

The culture in Miami Beach was not the type of atmosphere that I wanted to raise my son in. It was filled with so much ungodliness, greed, and lack of moral values on one end of the beach and on the other side were people who wouldn't talk to anyone who was outside of their religion. At the same time, I was becoming very fatigued. I had no energy at all. I thought that because of all the stress from the new changes going on was what was draining me. I had no gumption.

My friend visited us regularly before we moved near her. I would give her gas money to come down, so it wasn't a hardship on her. My son loved playing with her child. During one of our visits together I started discussing with her the stress that I was going through and that I wanted to get out of Miami Beach. We discussed again how I should move near her, so we could help each other out.

I was feeling terrible and I thought that I was just over-doing it. I felt like I couldn't catch up with myself no matter how much I rested, so my friend offered me one of her prescription pills. It was a medicine that she took to calm her nerves. So, I took the pill and it did help my system to calm down. Before she left to go back home she offered to give me a bottle with some pills in it. So, I took them, and I just kept the bottle in my drawer. I didn't want to take the pills because I have always been the type of person who didn't like taking a bunch of medications.

Prior to that I was starting to feel tremors in my body when I laid down. I wasn't sure if it was the ground that was vibrating where I lived since most homes didn't have basements. We did live near the beach, so I thought that maybe I was feeling aftershocks of some sort. For a while I just blew the symptoms off. I did have some health issues in Jersey, but I decided to eat better and work on my health while I was living in Florida. Yet, I didn't feel like myself not matter what I was doing to try and help my body be strengthened. So, one day I took the pills that my friend gave me out of the drawer and I took one. It took away the stress. So, I started taking them once a day.

I had some symptoms of thyroid problems before moving to Florida, but the doctor never suggested that I needed to go on medication for it. I tried natural things to boost my thyroid but then I completely forgot about the problem. I pressed through it all being the trooper that I am, and I concentrated on finding our new home instead. I didn't take what was happening too serious with my health.

In the meantime, I continued with the search to decide if I wanted to move closer to my friend. I thought it over and found out that it was so much cheaper and more affordable to move there. I prayed about it and decided that is what we will do, move near my friend's house so our kids can play together, and then we could settle down for good. So, I contacted a realtor and a banker and got the ball rolling. We finally found a home that we wanted to purchase and moved forward with all the paperwork.

I had to apply for a loan first and to get a loan for a house you must take care of your debts. That's what I had to do, get rid of some old debts from past credit accounts that I had completely forgotten about. I had to get letters from the creditors saying that I paid the balance on the credit cards that my ex and I had used and send it to the bank. It was frustrating. I must admit I was so excited at the idea of my son and I having our very own home for the first time ever that I worked through the frustration of it all until it finally got all cleared up.

It took a bit longer than what I expected. I believe there may have been a valid reason as to why I had a hard time. What I do think is that I may have missed seeing God blocking the deal and giving me a chance to change my mind so that I didn't move to that area. And even though I prayed about it, I was moving more in my flesh and selfish motives instead of really listening to God. Yet, I was adamant about getting a home. I wasn't ready to go back to Jersey and I wasn't sure I ever was.

After all the red tape got sorted out and my loan finally came through to go look for a house to purchase, I had received a letter in the mail from my friend stating that she no longer wanted to be friends with me. Even if I moved to her town. I thought it was odd that she was acting this way. Then I remembered that we had gotten into an argument a couple of weeks prior because I was concerned about her health and she got mad at me for it. This wasn't the first time I had received a letter like this from her either.

The real problem was that my friendship to her was genuine but her relationship to me was not. She had no problems taking my money as I willingly gave it to her. I also gave her $2,000.00 for her older daughter to put down on a car and instead she used it for herself to pay her own bills. I was a blessing to her out of love and she was cursing the friendship. I think in all honesty she was jealous of what I had.

I then decided that maintaining a relationship with her is not worth the trouble because I was under enough stress. How many know the enemy likes to pile things on you all at once? Or was this God trying to lead me in another direction? This so-called friend was the type of person who never had a problem receiving help from others but one thing I noticed about her was that she never gave back anything to anyone else unless something was in it for her. Realizing this helped me to cut off the relationship.

I never like to talk negative about people, but I need to explain here the difference between someone who is considered a real friend and someone who just uses people. Let's just set the record straight so that we see the whole picture. I helped her out so many times before we both lived in Florida. When she was struggling and had lost custody of her kids and had no place to go I took her in and gave her a place to live with my family. More than once. My family fed her and was patient with her until she got back on her feet again. She was a long-time friend so of course I was going to help her.

Once again, she needed help before the last time she left to move to another state and I let her live with me. When she moved and started getting herself some help, she supposedly found the Lord. She started to call herself a Christian and seemed to be doing better. I was so proud of her for getting help.

I then found out that we can be sober but still not have our mind renewed. That is what was happening here. Eventually I found out she just used the counselors to talk to when she needed to talk. And she told them the truth when it was convenient for her. I saw how she would hide the things going on in her home from the therapists when she didn't want them to know what was going on. I started to see her true colors.

That didn't deter me from moving near her because I accepted her for who she was knowing that she had issues. But after I received her letter in the mail stating that she didn't want to be friends anymore I honored her request. I realized that the relationship that I thought we had was just based on lies and greed. I decided not to speak with her anymore, but I did move to the place I had picked out because I had already started the process of buying my new home.

We finally moved into our new home and stayed in there for a couple of more years. During these years, they were a lonely time for me. My health was getting worse. I never met anyone as a partner and my son was only interested in playing with his friends now as he was no longer a little toddler. I was missing my real friends and family from back home. The holidays were not the same anymore. I had this great big house and I still felt alone. There were no parties and no people to celebrate birthdays and holidays with. My home felt empty. There was no family unit or friends to fill it up with laughter and joy. My son and his friends were basically all the company that we had in our home. Occasionally, I would hang out with my son's friend's mom or my neighbors. It just wasn't the same though. I didn't know them long enough to tell my inner secrets too.

To keep busy, I did activities with my son like going to his baseball games and volunteering at the snack bar. I took him to art classes and he even attempted dance classes. My only joy was raising him, but I also knew he was homesick. I saw the signs from God that maybe we should have left Florida sooner, but I didn't want to pay attention to them. I finally had the things that I've always wanted. A brand-new home, my bills were being paid, I had a new truck and peace, so I thought. I could go out and have fancy dinners with my son and buy us nice things. I didn't have to worry about not being able to take care of my son even though I wasn't receiving any child support. I had my own money to support us. I was well off. But my heart was still lonely. How is it that a person can have so much and still feel empty?

I was feeling weaker in my body as time passed. I couldn't ignore it anymore. I finally broke down and went to a doctor. He gave me different medicines to try to help alleviate some of my issues. Month after month I would revisit him, and it became the same routine but no results in my health. I had plenty of blood work and exams done which cost a fortune but nothing specific ever showed up. He had me on some heavy-duty medications. One of the pills that I was taking was the one that my friend had given to me, the doctor prescribed it for me to take. They just made me tired and want to sleep all the time. By this time, I was on a lot of medication.

One day I went in for my regular checkup and they told me that the doctor had died! What? Really? I said. They told me that he had a heart-attack. I couldn't believe it. My doctor had a heart attack? Go figure. So, they referred me to another doctor. One thing I have found out is that when you have money the doctors will almost agree to give you anything. It's a funny thing what money can do to people. I had found a woman doctor and she added another pill to my long list of medications already. I was so tired by the afternoon from the medicines that I would sleep while my son was in school and then stay awake until bed time. I felt my body just deteriorating. I was losing weight and my strength was expiring. I thought to myself am I dying? Why isn't anyone finding out what is wrong with me? Aside from my thyroid acting up and having infections all the time, no one had any answers.

I was now in the state of mind of being hopeless. My money was running out because of having to pay for doctors' visits and medications that were so expensive. I couldn't work because I was so sick all the time on top of being tired. It got to the point where I was beyond my capacity to realize a change needed to take place in my life. I couldn't understand why I was so sick, why I'm not meeting good friends, why we couldn't get settled into a good church? Nothing was coming together. As the money started to deplete I had applied for disability because that is the advice I was given. At this point I believed it. So, I applied, and they denied me. I went back to the guy who did the interview for my eligibility to ask him why he denied me. He said, "usually I don't tell people why I deny them but since you came back and want an answer I'll tell you.'" He said, "I don't believe that your life will always be this way." That's all he said to me. I left thinking what does he know? He can't possibly understand the physical and emotional pain that I've been through!

Times were getting tougher. One-night God said to me, "Sherri now that I have given you your heart's desire are you happy?" I said not really. He said, "Are you ready to fulfill the desires I have for you?" Then I broke down in tears because I knew that I had to give up the beautiful home that I just purchased and surrender this part of my life to Him. It didn't fulfill me, and I knew God was right. It didn't satisfy my soul or fill the deepest hurts. It only comforted me temporarily. It was all just material things. Then He said, "If you do this I will one day restore everything back to you." I heard Him so clearly through the tears. How could I refuse Him? He was the only One who kept me sane, who gave me hope and encouragement. So, I said okay.

I hired the same realtor that I bought my house from to sell it. Strange I know but true. God spoke again to me and said the first people coming to see the house will buy it and they did. After the house was sold you would have thought that I had learned my lesson and would have taken God's advice, but I didn't. I thought okay I will down grade and live more humbly. So, I bought a mobile home instead and I gave away everything that a mobile home could not house. All the brand-new things that I had bought to decorate my other home with I gave away to friends and the Salvation Army.

I thought God would be happy with that decision and that I gave away mostly everything in my home. I took what I could fit in the mobile home and made it cozy. For a while. But trouble was happening around me. I had a drunken neighbor who use to blast his music. Weird neighbors on the other side of us. And behind me people who liked to party every night. My one friend said not to move into that mobile home, but I did anyway. I was too frail to see all the things that God was trying to reveal to me and I believe that at this point I was so numb by all the medicines that I didn't care anymore.

All the signs were around me, but I wasn't paying attention, or should I say I didn't want to. I didn't want to return to the state that I had lived in where I just experienced the worst grief of my life. I didn't want to be back around the familiar settings and sad reminders just yet even though my heart was trying to heal emotionally. I was so sick physically, but I still wasn't convinced enough to leave Florida. I was being rebellious.

I was getting sicker and the medicines were not helping me. I needed financial help at this point, so I could maintain the rent. The women in the office where I lived were so gracious to help. I had no other income coming in except what was left in my checking account and being too sick to work I needed to find medical coverage for me and my son. I couldn't afford my medicines and the constant visits to the doctor anymore. I was on a sliding scale fee for a while at the clinic but that only lasted so long. When those resources ended, I was told to apply for government assistance. They told me I had too much money in the bank to receive help from them but if I spend the last of my money and became almost penniless they would help me. They said this when I only had $4,000.00 left to my name as my income for the year. Talk about a twisted scenario. So, I took the last of my money out of the bank, paid my bills and rent and bought food. Then when I was down to my last pennies they gave me assistance so me and my son could have medical coverage.

Day by day I was losing my strength. My current doctor suddenly stopped seeing me because now I had Medicaid. I couldn't believe it. I was referred to another doctor. I started seeing the new doctor and I thought that it was business as usual. But he questioned me as to why I was on all these types of medicines? He wasn't happy. He told me that he wanted me to be interviewed and assessed by another doctor. So, I agreed. The funny thing is that I went to this clinic looking for one specific doctor and she wasn't available, so I wound up seeing this other doctor. God had a plan so that I would listen this time.

I set up the appointment and went through an evaluation and then I waited. They gave me meds to hold me over until I came to my next appointment. I went to my next appointment and they said that they wanted me to see the Shrink as I call it. So, I did. I broke down telling him that I missed my family and that it was around the anniversary of my oldest son's death and that I felt sad about it all. I'll never forget the words he said to me. He said, "take a computer and look at it, it has different pictures on it, but you're not looking at the total picture." "The whole vision." But I got so upset at him for saying that to me as if he had no compassion. From that point on he wanted me to take pills for depression. I told him I'm not depressed, just stressed, and sad because I miss my family. He said take the script and decide what you want to do. He also wanted to switch one of my medicines, so that I could get off it and he gave me something else to replace it. I had made up my mind never to see him again

I left perturbed and annoyed because he was not only interrupting my daily routine at the time but was giving me what I felt like was a bunch of jargon. Even though I was looking for change I didn't want to do it the way he wanted me to. After leaving the session I went home and took a shower. While in the shower God said to me, "if you continue on the path you're on you will die." If I wasn't listening to Him before that statement, I certainly was listening now because I knew He was right. I could feel my body slipping in ways that I had never felt before and I was scared.

From that day forward, I decided that it was time to listen to the One who never led me astray and who always led me in the right direction. I started on this journey to ween myself from some of the medications that I was on. The first couple of meds were easy to stop and I felt fine with no symptoms of withdrawal. But then I decided to rid myself of the last one and do it cold turkey just like the other two, but it didn't go so well.

The problem I had with weaning off the last medication was that I didn't know you couldn't stop medications just like that! No one gave me instructions not to do that. And because it was in my system for a couple of years it didn't leave my body without a fight. I went off it too fast and I started to manifest terrible withdrawal symptoms. I would get headaches along with vomiting several times a day. I was hospitalized for dehydration from the vomiting about four times. I had constant diarrhea. I had insomnia and restlessness and as the medication left my body I could not feel my body parts. I thought that I had lost all feeling of sensory perception in my body. I would pinch myself and feel nothing. I thought it would never end.

I was so desperate for help that I wound up calling the frenemy. (My friend who didn't want to be my friend any longer). There was no one else who lived near me that I knew who could help me. I didn't want my son to see what I was going through and I needed help with driving him back and forth to school. I thank God for her kids who stepped in to help the most. She agreed to help me if she could use my truck. Remember I said she didn't doing anything unless there was something in it for her? At this point I didn't care. She helped for a week and then she invited me over to her house. I wasn't eating, just drinking some liquids. I decided to go to her home against my better judgment, but I was so sick. I knew that it wasn't the person that I wanted to be with but there was no one else to take care of my son. It wasn't long before she seemed inconvenienced by me, but she went on with her daily routines. She would ask me occasionally if I was ok. While I stayed at her house I had brought all my groceries over, so we would have food. Even while I was sick I did their dishes and their wash and would fold it. She didn't even appreciate that.

One day she drove me back home because we needed to check on my dogs. My one dog was so stressed from her company. She would leave my dogs on the porch for hours in the hot sun while she took a nap in my mobile home. I had to take my one dog to the vet to see if she was ok. They told me that my dog went into a fake pregnancy because her hormones were so stressed from this person. I couldn't believe it!

Back to when we were checking on the dogs that day. I felt as if I wanted to stay at my place, but she insisted that I come back to her house and sleep over. She said I could even sleep in her bed. It seemed odd that she was acting so nice to me because the whole time I was at her place she pretty much avoided me. She tried to convince me to admit myself into a place that had nothing but white walls and locked doors. It stunk like urine and looked like no one cleaned it. I thank God that I didn't commit myself. I didn't belong there, but she didn't care. She was annoyed that I didn't commit myself. So, she literally started an argument with me and was going to leave me in a store parking lot.

It wasn't enough that I was sick already and arguing with her but then I would go into the supermarket to get some items to buy and the other customers would stare at me because I had so many needle marks and bruises on my arms and hands from being in the hospital. The people thought I was a drug addict and a prostitute. I couldn't cover up the bruising because it was so hot out. I felt humiliated by people staring at me and nodding their heads in disgust as they judged me when they didn't even understand what was really happening to me. My so-called friend was doing the same thing. But I had to shrug it off. I was too ill to worry about one more thing.

I decided to go back to her place for one more night to be with my son and I just overlooked the fact that something seemed odd. Later that night I overheard a conversation she was having about me to her therapist. After she got off the phone I confronted her about it, but she denied it. I didn't feel right after that. I should have trusted my gut and went home. But I stayed because my son was enjoying being with her kids.

Then her older child took her younger child back to her place and wouldn't allow my son to go with them. That was strange to me. I knew that something was up but couldn't figure it out. I dismissed it and slept in the other room. In the morning, I waited for her to come back home with my truck. Suddenly I see her, and her therapist and another lady come walking up to the house. When they came into the house my frenemy told me that I had to take my son and leave her home. She treated me like I was someone who had broken into her house. She treated me like a stranger. I was so upset. It was then that I realized that she wanted to make a show out of me in front of her counselor. As if she needed to gain some brownie points with them. There was absolutely no reason for her to do that and especially in front of my son no less.

I grabbed all my things and my son and left. My last words to all of them were that they were not acting like true Christians and that there was no reason for the commotion that she made. Like I said she was a troubled person who only cared about herself. The funny thing is that I met with her counselor before I even moved near her and in a non-challan way she warned me about her. Be careful who you trust! Listen to your gut instincts.

I could have avoided all of this if I would have just gone back to NJ when God instructed me to. At least I would have been surrounded by people who loved me and who would have had our best interest in mind. Not everyone who calls themselves a Christian, acts like one. Not everyone who says they're your friend is. You need to go with your gut instincts and follow that lead it will spare you a lot of unnecessary turmoil. Not everyone is truly your friend no matter how long you have known them! Look at the signs that are signaling loudly around you carefully because they just may be leading you in another direction.

Lesson Learned: God has methods that can be contrary to people's ideas of the way things should play out. At times, we don't understand them and may not like the answers on how we should change a situation. Which are because He does things in different ways than we would think of doing them. So, it isn't comfortable for us when we're trying to get our minds to come around to seeing His point of view on how to bring that change into our lives. We have a certain way of doing things, so we want to continue doing them the same way. The problem with that is there is no real solution happening. No healing that is taking place and we continue to still get entrapped in these same situations. We don't want to do it another way because it takes the control away from us and gives it to someone else. But don't you know that when things are out of control and you can't see things for what they truly are for yourself, someone else needs to? God was the only One seeing how out of control I was. He even made sure to speak clearly through all the mess that I was going through. And when I didn't listen the first time, He made sure to speak repeatedly to me. How kind is that? That's why it's important to listen to that inner voice. It's there for a specific purpose. It's an indicator that gives us direction towards a better option than the present condition that we're currently in and trying to get free from. What I've learned is that the more I discipline myself to listen when I first hear that inner voice and act upon what I've heard the first time, I find myself getting out of something a lot quicker than if I did it on my own without listening. It's not the easiest process by far but it is something that you can certainly obtain over time with great success. Let's face it we all need a sounding board. Especially at our lowest points in life. The question is why not God's help? Especially when no one else is there to help. I was so medicated, yet He wasn't willing that I would die that way. Even as a Christian as I was wandering away from His love He still made sure that I heard Him speaking. He was even using the enemy in my life to help me and beyond that He was using her to show me what real friends are not! It was a hard lesson to learn. It hurt! The funny thing is that He still used my enemy to help me in my time of need. Now only God can orchestrate that. The truth is that I took myself down a path that I knew was wrong. I let my flesh rule over my spirit life and that is where I made my errors. I saw the signs from the moment I started not feeling well and all the trouble I had to go through to get a loan for the house and then my frenemy's letter. Way back in the beginning of this whole situation I could have avoided a lot of heartache and wasted time. Stubbornness will not lead us to any solutions. It may even take us further off course like it did me. Don't waste your precious time. Listen to God. He will never lead you into darkness because He only consists of the light. Yes, He will be with us in our dark times but I'm sure He prefers us not to walk into chaos willingly. Let's be what He thinks we should be and that is a people that are growing in His goodness and who are wanting what He wants. What He wills for our lives is so much grander than what we can even imagine. Let's let Him love us into wholeness so that we can help others out of the mess that we have been through, so they don't have to struggle or miss Him, when He is speaking to them. There is a great reward for those who seek God and believe that He is who He says He is. If you're in a certain situation right now that is holding you back, then take an inventory of what you have seen or felt that seems out of order but have disregarded. Go back over what you inventoried and see where maybe your lacking that missing puzzle piece to get you back on track. Anything that you overlooked and just found will be the answer to finding your solution. God is more than willing to help you on your way because He has great plans for you. Write down when you believe you heard God's voice and what He was telling you and link the messages together. Recollect the signs you saw and link them together. God will work everything together for you if you just apply yourself to obeying His voice.

Psalm 18:30 – God's way is perfect. All the Lord's promises prove true. He is a shield for all who look to Him for protection.

Chapter 15- Deciding to Finally Go Home
(I don't want to die)

All my faculties were starting to slowly come back to my body and mind now, so I made the decision to leave Florida. I knew that if I stayed in Florida that I would be making the wrong decision. I would die there. Through all the pain and suffering that was going on I could still hear the voice of God giving me directions through it all. He is so amazingly gracious and a good Father. I could never blame God for what was happening to me because it was my decisions that brought me to the place where I was. He just wanted to get me out of that place because I wasn't voluntarily doing it. He needed to redirect me onto a right path. He knew that continuing to hear His voice was what it was going to take so that I would make the decision to go back home. Deep down I knew if I accepted His direction that there would be a better outcome for my life. So, I decided to start listening to Him again. Even though I didn't completely understand it at the time. We don't always have to understand why we're being led in another direction, but we should follow His lead for a better result.

I put my property up for sale and then slowly started to pack our things. It was not easy for me because I was not well, but the grace of God was sufficient for me to complete the task. He gave me the strength to make it through. After all this was His plan. After packing most of our belongings, I sent a bunch of boxes back to NJ. I gave away all the new furniture that I had bought for my mobile home and blessed a woman who had finally moved into her first home with it all. I just wanted to get rid of everything and go back home.

Remember, God told me that if I stayed in Florida that I wouldn't live for much longer. I obeyed His advice. My gut told me that if the property was sold quickly that I was truly following Gods lead. You know how we are as humans, we want signs. It only took one person who came, looked at my property once again and then he bought it. I knew I was moving forward and doing the right thing even while I wasn't well. It's in our weakness that God is made strong through us. He wants to see us succeed! He doesn't want the enemy to win our souls. God will do everything He can to get us to reach our destiny. The important part of this process for me was that I was moving gradually towards a different path. It was crucial to my well-being. I didn't realize how critical it was until I returned home.

The day finally arrived when it came time to load up only our most valuable things and leave. Anything else that was left behind was given to friends. Our truck was packed to the very top of the roof and mind you we had two dogs with us. We were so cramped, but we didn't care we were so excited to be leaving Florida. My son couldn't wait to leave. I handed over the keys to the new owner and we were on the road heading for the next chapter in our lives.

We made it safely back home! I could have kissed the ground when I got out of my truck. We were so filled with joy as we saw the welcome to NJ sign and the first thing we did was go and see my mom at her work. When we saw her, all we did was cry happy tears. It felt so good to be home. I had forgotten how much I truly missed this place. I knew I was healed when I felt the emotions of love and safety again instead of heartache and pain from when we first left. We all went home and reminisced about what was going on in each other's lives. I also got to catch up with my friends whom I had missed so dearly. What a homecoming we had! I could feel the healing process continuing to take place and I knew that life had to get better from here.

After we settled in, I found a doctor. I needed someone who could figure out what was going on with me and why I was not getting well. I was praying but I still was not getting any answers. I started the intense process of having blood work done. I had been tested for so many things that I was beginning to feel like a pin cushion. When the results started to come back to the doctor he thought it was just the Epstein-Barr virus attacking my body. So, they treated me accordingly, but I still did not get well, I was only getting worse. I knew God had a plan, so I had to hang in there as tough as it was. I wanted answers and I wanted to live. I trusted Gods lead and kept praying.

Amid me having to continuously go back and forth to the doctor because I kept on getting sick and needed antibiotics all the time it was then that they decided it was time for more testing. This time a new assistant joined the practice and she assessed me. She added to my portfolio that my thyroid had been failing. So, we started to discuss options for treating that. Then the doctor came in and said no he didn't think that was the issue. So, on and on this continued. I was just being treated as the symptoms kept arising. Then that assistant left, and another new nurse practitioner started to evaluate me. She was determined to find out what was wrong.

At this point I was so sick that my organs felt like they were shutting down. My heart was acting crazy and I had no strength what so ever, it was getting to the point that if they didn't find out soon what was happening I knew I was going to die. God wasn't kidding when He told me to get back to NJ. After many more antibiotics and many trips back to get blood work done my doctor finally found something, it was Lyme's Disease! So, they started me on another course of powerful antibiotics for 30 days, then 60 and then 90 days. The first 30 to 60 days the antibiotics were not working. Which caused them to make the treatment time go a little longer. This still was not working either. I thought we finally had an answer, but this was not it. I begged God to help. I was so desperate. I knew He was there with me because I could see His hand in my situation, I wasn't dead yet. Besides, I had too many things left to do on this Earth and one of them was the completion of this book! Even while I was sick I continued to write ¾ of this book.

I had to get several other tests done on my brain, my back, and my heart. I decided that I was going to do it so that I could see the whole picture. Everything came back mostly normal with a few exceptions to what was going on with me. The doctors thought some of the results were not necessarily related to the Lyme's, so they disregarded those test results. I did decline to do a spinal tap test. I didn't see the need for that. I felt like we were pulling at straws now. If you could have seen my calendar, there was nothing but doctor's appointments to fill up my schedule. I was seeing all kinds of different specialist's. It was becoming overwhelming. I don't know how I did it all except for the grace of God on my life.

As I saw one specialist she had told me that one of my results came back stating that I had some white spots on my brain then another specialist said that it was nothing. It was frustrating and all I could do was cry. I had faith, but my flesh was so weak. I'll be honest sometimes I just wanted to leave this Earth and go onto glory and this was one of them times. Then I saw another specialist who was an Infectious Disease doctor who believed that I had not been diagnosed in enough time and I was now in the late stages of Lyme's. She had decided at this point that the only vital treatment for me was to be put into a hospital and have a port inserted into my arm. This was called a pic line which had a tiny tube running from my arm down into my heart so that the antibiotics could directly reach my system.

I was hesitant to do this treatment, but I finally agreed. I mean putting something down into my arm and reaching near my heart was so scary to think about and to top it off, I was to be awake for the whole procedure. I thought about it and decided that there weren't many other options left and let's be honest here I did not receive a miracle yet. I got the procedure done and then I had to have the shipments of medicine delivered to my home every week. I also had to have a visiting nurse come and check the site and clean it every week so that it didn't get infected.

In between her visits I had to administer the antibiotic through a syringe to the port and then flush it after I was done. I had a mesh pad that served as a covering and had to keep it covered all the time. I had to make sure that it was clean all the time so that I didn't contract any other infections. This went on for 28 days straight. It was hard day after day dealing with this whole situation.

My mother, son and I lived together. They had to see me go through this ordeal day after day and my mother would cry. It was by no means easy on them. My son held everything in and was angry at times. I knew it couldn't have been easy for either one of them to see this happening to me. It wasn't easy for me, so I can only image what they were feeling. They didn't say much about it they just wanted me to get better.

I decided not to tell everyone what was going on. Not out of pride but because I didn't want the pity, or the attention drawn to me and away from God. I was sure that He was going to get me through this just like He had gotten me through the death of my son and the divorce. If He stuck with me through all of that I knew He wasn't leaving me now. I'm not going to lie, I struggled with this whole dilemma because my body seemed to be failing me, but I found my strength in God to keep my spirit strong. I wanted to get well. I had so many things in my heart that I wanted to see happen in my life. Like seeing my younger son grow up and graduate and drive his first car. I didn't get to see that with my older son. I knew that what God had promised me concerning the future needed to still happen. I also wanted to eventually get married again one day. None of these things happened yet and I knew God wasn't a liar. He had already done so much to see me through. I trusted Him with my life literally.

After the treatment was over I started to work on recouping my body. I had to take medicine for my thyroid because of the Lyme's. It took quite some time to get myself back into shape. The after effects of the Lyme's were severe, so I had to make the necessary dietary changes and rest continually. I had body aches, inflammation and joint pain that stemmed from the disease and I was struggling with some memory issues. But with a lot of prayer and seeking God for my healing I got well. I am not like I used to be but I'm not as worse as I was. My immune system was compromised because I didn't know what was wrong with me for so long because it went undiagnosed for several years and covered up by medications. The bacteria just ravaged my body.

God has literally healed me in so many areas that no doctor could. I continued to work and go to church during my treatments. I refused to give up. Today I refuse to give up as well. I am not nearly as bad as some of the Lyme's cases out there. I have friends and co-workers who literally have been physically and mentally challenged by this disease to the point where they are now disabled and on tons of medications. So, although God did not deliver me from everything all together, He has made me whole, sober minded, and in good health so that I may see His promises happen in my life. He has taught me ways to stay healthy. One of those ways was to maintain intimacy with Him daily and to remain in His presence for hours at a time.

There have been many other things that I have had to deal with due to the Lyme's disease through out these many years since I have been treated even up to completing this book. I had to see a gynecologist because they thought that I may have had cancer of the uterus, but God said no! I struggled with constant infections. Once again, I literally thought I was going to die. I was in and out of the emergency room for a couple of weeks and then admitted to the hospital because once again through bloodwork they couldn't figure out what was wrong with me. I was literally losing weight and not eating due to the severe vomiting and diarrhea that I was having. I lost 45 pounds within a month and could not eat anything but baby food and drink water. I had to have several tests done which all came back quite normal. They didn't find cancer or any other major disease. During this illness, the doctors had me on about 10 medications just to keep me out of the hospital. So, I could go back to work.

They finally decided to give me a pill that was for the small bowel. It was an antibiotic that targeted an excessive growth of bad bacteria in the small intestines. That was the thing that started the healing process. Along with dietary changes, once again I was able to get my health back within a few months.

This time for real I literally I thought I was going home to be with the Lord. I could not function mentally or physically. I still held onto the promises of the Lord. He is faithful. I knew there were things that still needed to be done before I left this Earth. The Lord preserved me once again. I was determined to make it through no matter what it took. Even though at times, I have to say that I was doubting. I was asking the Lord to take me home to Heaven. Yet He helped me once again maintain my sanity by getting me to take another path. This time it was to focus on other things. He used a beautiful park for me to go walking in day after day. Sometimes twice a day to walk the perimeter and watch his wildlife and creation as He spoke to me and strengthened me through this terrible journey. He did this to take the focus of the problem off my mind and onto His love. He allowed me to have this intimacy with Him one on one, He allowed me to cry out to Him as His presence and voice consoled me. The more I sought Him the more He would heal me.

This is what He used to help heal me. We do not work like God does we don't think like He does until we put on the mind of Christ. Then we get wisdom, knowledge, and strength to push forward. The bible is true when it says God will never leave us or forsake us. It is only when we stop looking for Him and cut off His voice that we don't find Him. I knew God was the only one who was going to bring me through this once again.

It doesn't end there. Right before wrapping up this book my best friend who was my doggie died and my son was in a car accident. I have been tried and tested repeatedly. After all that I have been through you would think that I'd be in a mental facility or dead by now, but God! This is where we find out how big our faith is and how strong we are. We find out how much our faith has grown and how much we have matured by how far we've come. We find out where our true strength and real weaknesses lie. We find out that God not only heals but He also does miracles.

This book was written so that you may find your purpose and strength in God no matter what you are facing. He is a God of Love. He is a good Father. I want you to know and see Him at work in my life so that you know of this truth that He maintains His faithfulness even when we are struggling. He is a forgiving God. He sent His son Jesus to die for the whole world. I must admit I couldn't even imagine being nailed to a wooden cross and hanging on it for hours with my flesh ripping off while trying to take each breathe in before it was my last, just to save humanity.

The last chapter in this book is my favorite. Yes, the testimonies of being an overcomer are wonderful but testifying of God is my real joy. I want to show you Him and how He heals and how He releases the supernatural in our lives so that we may know that He is real beyond any shadow of a doubt. After you read these accounts I'm going to pray for you so that you too will experience Gods love for yourself. My prayer is that He will visit you face to face so that you too can have this intimacy with Him that will carry you through the darkest times of your life.

Lesson Learned: The struggle is seriously real folks. I know I have been down this road more times than I'd care to admit. We never pretend that sickness and death do not exist. Yet, we must look to the one who brings us lasting results and His name is God. What I have learned is that humans are limited in their knowledge and thinking. Both doctors and any other kind of practitioner. They can only go so far in the type of treatments that they can offer us. They don't have all the answers to our problems and half the time they can't even diagnose a source of illness to properly treat. That's why God holds all the answers. He is otherworldly and has solutions that mankind has no idea about. He has the supernatural touch if you will to transform any situation into a testimony of His goodness. He is love, and He loves us. He wants to see us healed and made whole both on the inside and the outside of this earthly body. He came that we may have life and have it more abundantly. He never created the world and all its inhabitants so that we could live a miserable and defeated life. He didn't spare His own life so that we could be defeated. What kind of God would that be? That's what I've learned from God the most. How to seek His face increasingly for my answers. He never stays silent for long and He always reveals a solution. Sometimes it comes in ways that we would never expect but never the less it comes. He has methods and ways that us humans cannot even conceive of. He is far more genius than any human being, yet He is so gracious to meet us where we are at when our body or minds seem to be failing us. He is supernatural. Unexplainable. He imparts to us the means to get wisdom and to find out the formulas for cures and different ways to help humanity take care of itself. He has purposed in us to invent and re-create like He does. He has given us the ability to reach certain plateaus in life. He has even caused some humans to be geniuses. But if we knew all that He did we would not need Him, would we? His ways are higher than our ways and so are His thoughts. That's why He says come unto me all that are weary, and I will give you rest. He says through Him we are strengthened. He understands that we cannot solve all of humanities frailties. In even all our best human efforts to try to do so. We will never come up with miracles, signs and wonders like God does. Yet, He never expects us to give up on ourselves either. That is why it is so important to understand that when your time is not up yet then you must continue to press in for your healing and your miracles. I have been healed and seen miracles numerous times. Not only in my own life but also in my families lives. God has the means to release supernatural provision from the Heavens to refresh and replenish our bodies and minds. He is no joke. But we must have a desire for His touch. We must continuously tap into the main power source and yearn for the one who loves us. You may be saying, Sherri you lost your son and your marriage, and you've been sick so much, how can you say that God is good, and He is love when all this has happened to you? My friends it is because of who He is and not who I am. It is because His enemy is my enemy on this Earth, yet He defends me from my enemies and gives me the power to defend myself. We are not without hope or solutions. The enemy never wanted me to write this book or get it published. That is why so much has come against me in my lifetime. But that is okay because God has had my back the whole time. In the next chapter, which is my favorite chapter of this book, you will see why I want to introduce you to Him. If you don't know Him or you want to get closer to Him, you can see for yourself why intimacy with God is so important. It is the solution to this life! I'm here to gladly share that with you.

Psalm 73:26 – My health may fail, and my spirit may grow weak, but God remains the strength of my heart; He is mine forever.

Chapter 16- God Sees Me Differently

When I started to realize who I wasn't, and I started to see through God's eyes who I really was meant to be, it was then that I gave myself permission to take new chances in life. Now I'm not going to lie here and tell you that it has been a bed of roses because it hasn't been. It's taken a lot of hard work, persistence, and great effort to stay well and become the woman I am today. It didn't happen overnight. It was a very long process but the key to the process is not giving up on yourself! The solution to every problem is knowing the power of God that believes in you. You see to make faith operate in your life you need to know that God goes before you to make the crooked places straight. When you realize that He is already two steps ahead of you and that He is waiting there, it is then that you will have the courage to move forward no matter what comes your way. But you must believe this truth first.

The scriptures in the bible weren't written so that the book could sit on a shelf and not be used. The bible is supernatural and powerful and can help each one of us get our head straightened out. The problem is that we don't want to take the time to read it! You must get to know God. You must have a balance in your walk. When I learned this truth, I gained great wisdom from God that has kept me out of trouble. From staying close to Him I have avoided many disasters and have only escalated in my life in obtaining a better one.

I have been able to raise my son properly because I was sober. I've obtained a career. I went to college to better my education and my job pay so that I could take care of my family properly. It was much better than living off the government. I used to hate having to go down to a crime ridden, drug infested city just to keep an appointment with the government so that I could get food stamps to help feed my son. It was an awful experience. It was needed at the time while I was growing in the Lord but when I regained my strength I knew it was time for something better. God wants us to achieve goals and live better he doesn't want to see us poor and suffering. That is not the gospel that I read about. My God is a King who lives in a kingdom and He has provided many opportunities for us to obtain to create success. You must be willing to do the work. You must start looking through the lens of Heaven and believe that every promise God has spoken to you about must still happen! If it hasn't happened yet, then let that be a great indicator that you are still in the battle and you must pursue to overcome. It will happen don't grow weary in well doing. When you're going through, it is the perfect time for your faith to expand! Your job is not to faint! Run your race for the prize of the high calling. Everyone in Heaven is routing you on for you to fulfill your destiny. So, go for it. Amen!

Lesson Learned: Because of the Lord's love for me I could become a better woman. I could take care of my son and raise him on my own. My mind had a chance to get renewed and change for the better. I can share this wisdom with others only because I went through the changes needed to get me to this place. I got to see that life is full of chances and promotions and that I had every right to them if I was willing to participate. God has a way of elevating you to the higher levels of life just by you getting to know Him and by spending the time trying to understand the plans that He has for your life. The plans that we have are often not the same plans that He has. So, we need to step back and realize when we are heading down the wrong paths whether it is in a job, relationship's, or money matters. The fact of the matter is truth wins every time. Lies are deceitful. And unbelievably we can lie to ourselves about life. We don't even have to have someone else do it for us. That is why having a relationship with God is so vital to our success. He only wants to see us proclaim the victory every time. You cannot say no. You cannot give up on yourself so easily and you must not let others persuade you onto a path that is not designed for you. You will know when it's not by the uncomfortable feelings you get. When you're not satisfied with anything in your life when things are boring and there is no joy. God wants us to come out on the other end knowing what we have just come through and getting the experience that we need to never go that route again and to help others along the way. Your life matters because others need you. You must respect yourself enough to say no to the things that are obstacles and that includes people. You must say yes to the risks ahead and let fear take a back seat. You'll never know what you can do if you keep missing opportunities that are presented to you. Will it be easy? No. Is it possible to live a whole other life? Absolutely. I'm living proof that it is. I'm ready for the next chapter in my life. I continue to learn new things about myself daily. I get to decide if I want to live with certain things in my life or not. Someone else doesn't get to choose that for me. We must become the leaders of our destiny. What good would it be to go through life always sad, miserable, disappointed, abused, poor, etc. That is not an abundant life. An abundant life doesn't mean one without trouble or trials it means that you have the scars to prove that you're an overcomer! Draw for yourself a strategic plan that is filled with purpose and hope. That brings fruit not only into your life but for the people around you as well. Together as we heal we can help others heal with the redeeming quality and supernatural power that God entrusts us with!

Galatians 5:1 – So Christ has truly set us free. Now make sure that you stay free, and don't get tied up again in slavery to the law.

Chapter 17- HIM

All the traumatic events that have occurred in my life, the alcohol, drugs, and illicit sex that I was doing all led me to dead end streets. It was only when I was introduced to God that my whole life started to have meaning again. Even through all the chaos that I experienced I could manage through every storm knowing that He was the one in control and I was not. I wasn't very good at managing my life when I was out of control. Someone had to be there guiding me.

I want to share with you the experiences that I have had with God to show you how real He truly is. You have read about some of them already but there are many more. These glimpses and supernatural experiences have kept my heart full and confident in knowing that when I saw God at work in my life I knew I couldn't fail. It was impossible. He was always present and never willing to give up on me during the best and worst times of my life.

Through Him teaching me great wisdom I could be a successful mother while being single. I made sure that I didn't compromise God's direction and love when I was raising my son. And even though he is nineteen now and able to make his own decisions I know that I have done my job well. Yes, my son did get spankings and I don't apologize for it. I know that if he didn't get them that he would probably be a lot worse off now as a person. I used to feel bad about it but now I realize that due to the lack of a father figure being in his life, it was the only way to make sure he knew what he could and couldn't get away with. Sometimes words aren't enough because we can go back on our word.

God would tell me or show me things that my son did, and I would confront him. He knew that I had this supernatural connection with God. He used to tell me not to pray for certain things because it would change everything. That's the power of a praying mother. My son has experienced the very supernatural acts of God himself. One day I was gathering up all the change that I had left in my change jug, so I could pay our phone bill. They were getting ready to shut our phone off. I would keep change in the jug for such emergencies until I got paid or if we needed food. The money that was in the jug was all that I had left until I got paid. Every penny mattered.

After I had counted out just enough money from the jug to pay the phone bill with, I put it in the envelope. I stuck it in my hand and ran out the door to pick up my younger son from the school bus. After I picked up my son we headed to the place where I could pay the phone bill. When I went to find the bill to pay it, I could not find the envelope with the money in it. I lost it! I quickly put my son in the car and I drove back to the places that I had been prior to that. We also returned home to see if I had dropped it on my way out, but we could not find it. I started to freak out because I could not understand where could it have gone?

At this point I was so upset because I didn't have any other money that I could use to pay the bill with and it was due that day. I ran upstairs so I could cry. I didn't want my son to see how upset I was. In a matter of minutes, we heard a noise come from the mail slot in our door. When the mail was delivered, you would hear the clang of the metal against the door. That's what we heard. So, we knew what that sound meant. I started running down the steps and then to my right I saw my younger son who was only age five or six years old at the time, on his knees, bent down by the couch and he was praying.

I ran with tears in my eyes towards the door and as I looked down there was the envelope that I had lost. The phone bill and all the money were in it. I quickly opened the door to thank the person who had delivered the envelope back to us but there was no one there. I looked both ways, up and down the street and in every direction and there was no one around! Not one soul. God had heard my son's prayers and sent supernatural help to us. The prayers of our children are powerful!

Another time I was at a store with my children and as we were approaching the car a man came from out of nowhere and tried to steal my pocketbook. I wasn't having it. I didn't have much and what I did have he was not going to take. As I struggled with this man I punched him in the nose as we were grappling and suddenly I could feel this enormous being behind me, His presence was so tangible that I knew someone was there. As soon as I felt this presence a horn sounded in the parking lot and the guy ran off. Without my pocketbook and we were all safe. How good is God. He had sent angelic help to aide me. I have had many encounters of angelic help.

I remember before I was saved how God delivered me from what could have been a premature death. I was hanging out with this guy. I used to date his friend but when I stopped dating him I was still friends with a person we will call Tom. Tom and I were strictly friends. I used to hang out with him when I wasn't hanging out with my other friends. One night he gave me some LSD. So, I took it. During the night, we had run into a few of his other friends. I started to feel strange around him I wasn't sure why because I had never felt that way before. It was getting late so we all decided that we were going to head home. I used to let him drive my car when we were partying. As we approached my car I got into the passenger side and he grabbed my head and it almost hit the car door window. He was very aggressive, and I said to him what are you doing? He blew it off as if it was an accident. I didn't really hang out with him after that night. Years later I read about him in the newspaper and how he had taken a girl home and killed her. I know that night God was watching over me so that the enemy did not have his way!

Another friend and I went to New York for a conference and we literally time traveled. We had prayed because we were lost, and it was very late. It was then that God supernaturally transported us home within a shorter time than what it would have originally taken us. We skipped a whole city.

Another time I was taking care of a client. I had to do an overnight shift. I slept in the client's guest room. I hardly had any sleep because by the time the client went to bed it was like four in the morning. I was beginning to doze off when I felt my spirit starting to lift out of my body and I heard a voice clearly say, "No, it's not time yet!" I knew that I had just had an out of body experience. I know they are real. It was quite strange as I could feel the pull of gravity as I was starting to leave my body and then was immediately sucked back in.

I have had so many experiences that are too many to write down here, but I will give you one last one. Last year I had walked out into my kitchen and suddenly, a transparent object that looked iridescent and opaque with a tint of the most beautiful blue I have ever seen appeared on my curtains. It is so hard to describe because it was other worldly. It opened like a vortex does and then it quickly shut itself up and disappeared.

I'm sharing these stories with you so that you can know there is a whole other world out there that belongs to you! It is where we originally come from. It is our home. It's called Heaven. I want to invite you into this supernatural place so that you can experience it for yourself. God wants to have that one on one contact with you. The supernatural is happening all around us we just need to open our spiritual senses up to experience it.

Lesson learned: I've learned that God is real. Heaven is real. The supernatural is real. And these things have contributed to my well-being. No one person or thing is more necessary for my life than God. He is my healer, sustainer, provider, husband, best friend, etc. I wouldn't be here right now if it wasn't for Him. God is someone that I can talk about for hours. I can even share His love with you. But the best way for you to get to know Him is by experiencing Him yourself. He has taught me how to love people in the right way and how to see life from His eyes instead of from my distorted views. He taught me how to rely on Him to get through life's delicate moments. I've learned how He is so patient with me. He helped me to rebuild my life and has brought me out of drug and sexual addictions. He didn't stop there! He took me from being broken hearted and rejected and made me feel loved and wanted. He showed me the purpose for my existence on this Earth and He continues to give me chance after chance to radiate His love to others. I'm still not perfected yet but I'm on my way. I pray my friends as you have read this book that you are being transformed already. That you are letting go of any baggage or negative circumstances that have held you back from your full potential. I really hope you feel loved. I hope you want to meet God now if you have never done so before. He is so willing to meet you. It's time that we re-navigate our souls to a solid foundation so that we can live the life we have always wanted to live and become who we have always wanted to be. There are no limitations with God. Sometimes we are like the caterpillar. It has it's struggles until it becomes a new creation. When the new creation comes, which is a butterfly then it's whole perception is changed and the butterfly soars. The caterpillar must shut itself away and remold it's being to come out as a new creation. Once it does it enjoys the nectars of this life. The symbolic meaning of the butterfly is to be born again. Do you want that? All the hard work it takes to create a beautiful you, are worth it to Him. God doesn't make junk, nor does He waste anything. In my last chapter, I want to invite you to meet Him for yourself so that you can have amazing encounters face to face with God!

Romans 8:18 – Yet what we suffer now is nothing compared to the glory He will reveal to us later.

Chapter 18- The Invitation of a Lifetime

Precious friend, let me tell you how you will never regret that you picked up this book or that you have received an invitation of a lifetime. God wants to meet you face to face. One on one. He wants to be completely consumed by you and wants to love you unconditionally. He will be with you on your best days as well as your worst days. He will give you joy and comfort you through any heartache. Just confess Him in your heart and He will be forever with you. Let me lead you into a prayer that you can audibly pray to God.

Father God, I want to know you. I want to be a part of your world and I want to enter Heaven when I die. I want to know you now. I'm asking for a personal relationship with you by acknowledging the finished work on the cross. I believe that you sent your son Jesus to die on that cross for me taking all my sin and shame. I confess every sin that has held me back from receiving my best life now. I want to see you face to face now God. I believe that Jesus died and rose again which gives me the victory in every area of my life. I apply Jesus blood over my life and to any hindrances from me prospering now. Your word says that you came so that I could have an abundant life so please show me how to do that. I receive the power of your Holy Spirit to come and dwell inside my mortal body so that you may guide me by your wisdom all the days of my life. God, I ask you to heal any areas that need it, whether it is spiritually, physically, or emotionally. I give you permission to break off every chain and negative mindset that keeps me from seeing the beauty of this life that you have given me. Take me as your child and adopt me into the family of God. In Jesus name, I pray this prayer. I am born again from above. Amen!

Lesson Learned: I have never regretted my decision to accept God into my life! I have gone from being a victim to a Victor! From brokenness to wholeness. From insecure to confident. From being rejected to knowing I am loved! The lesson learned here is that I am the best version of myself and I am becoming the woman that I have always wanted to be. I can love myself and others and because of that I glorify God with my life. You can too! Start a new journey to wellness today. Start to rebuild your life with God! Pray, meditate, and never stop asking God to come and visit you face to face. I want to recommend a book to you. Face to Face appearances from Jesus. By David E. Taylor. This book will change your life. If you want to get closer to God, let this be the next book you read! You won't regret it my friend.

Hebrews 10:35-36 – So do not throw away this confident trust in the Lord. Remember the great reward it brings you! 36- Patient endurance is what you need now, so that you will continue to do God's will. Then you will receive all that He has promised.

About the Author

I am just a humbled woman by the grace of God. A single mom who gave birth to two children, lost one, survived divorce, struggled with illness and was left to die at times. My aspirations as a little girl were to live out the American dream but that was not God's plan for my life. As I navigated through many trials and storms each of them has revealed to me the answers as to why my dream never happened that way. *This* is my story. I have been given access to a whole new vision for my life. It's Gods vision. I give Him all the glory for me being an Author. This book was written from all the wisdom He has entrusted to me. Now I give it to you~

With all my love,

~Sherri~

61365247R00130

Made in the USA
Middletown, DE
10 January 2018